····· **PREFACE** ·····

Learning to play a musical instrument is one of the most satisfying experiences a person can have. Being able to play along with other musicians makes that even more rewarding. This collection of Disney songs is designed to make it easy to enjoy the fun of gathering with friends and family to make music together.

The selections in this book include a wide variety of Disney songs drawn from several generations. These songs will provide fun opportunities to make music with other players. The music for each song displays the chord diagrams for five instruments: ukulele, baritone ukulele, guitar, mandolin and banjo. The chord diagrams indicate basic, commonly used finger positions. More advanced players can substitute alternate chord formations.

It is easy to find recordings of all these tunes performed by outstanding musicians. Listening can help you understand more about the style as you and your friends play these songs.

The following songs are the property of:
Bourne Co.
Music Publishers
www.bournemusic.com

Baby Mine
Give a Little Whistle
Heigh-Ho
Hi-Diddle-Dee-Dee (An Actor's Life for Me)
I'm Wishing
I've Got No Strings
Some Day My Price Will Come
When I See an Elephant Fly
When You Wish Upon a Star
Whistle While You Work

Arranged by Mark Phillips

ISBN 978-1-70518-196-6

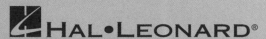

Visit Hal Leonard Online at
www.halleonard.com

World headquarters, contact:
Hal Leonard
7777 West Bluemound Road
Milwaukee, WI 53213
Email: info@halleonard.com

In Europe, contact:
Hal Leonard Europe Limited
1 Red Place
London, W1K 6PL
Email: info@halleonardeurope.com

In Australia, contact:
Hal Leonard Australia Pty. Ltd.
4 Lentara Court
Cheltenham, Victoria, 3192 Australia
Email: info@halleonard.com.au

*Based on the "Winnie the Pooh" works, by A. A. Milne and E. H. Shepard

Standard Ukulele

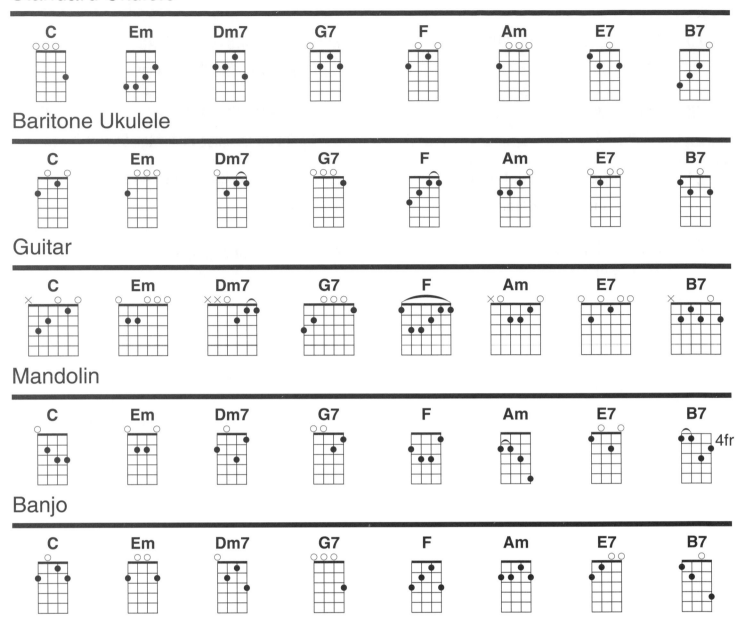

Baritone Ukulele

Guitar

Mandolin

Banjo

Baby Mine

from DUMBO

Words by Ned Washington
Music by Frank Churchill

Verse
Moderately slow

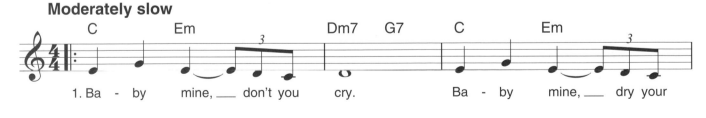

1. Ba - by mine, ___ don't you cry. Ba - by mine, ___ dry your

eye. Rest your head close to my heart, nev - er to part, ba - by of

mine.   2. Lit - tle   one, ___ when you play,   don't you mind ___ what they

say.   Let those eyes spar - kle and shine, nev - er a tear, ba - by of

Bridge

mine.   If they knew sweet lit - tle you,   they'd end up lov - ing you

too.   All those same peo - ple who scold you,

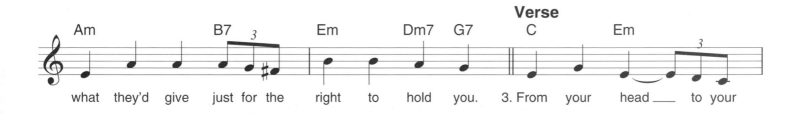

Verse

what they'd give just for the right to hold you. 3. From your head ___ to your

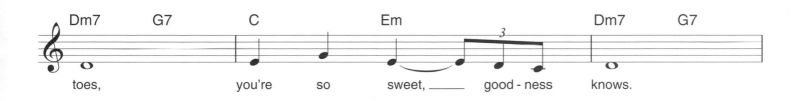

toes,   you're so sweet, ___ good - ness knows.

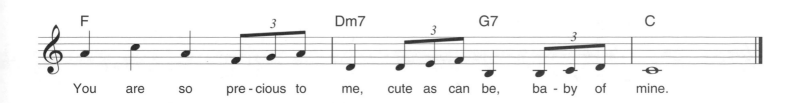

You are so pre - cious to me, cute as can be, ba - by of mine.

Standard Ukulele

Baritone Ukulele

Guitar

Mandolin

Banjo

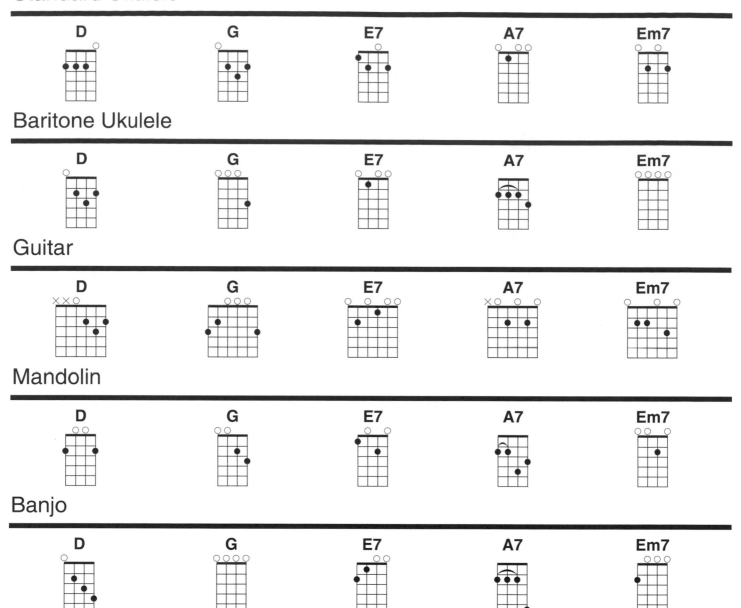

The Ballad of Davy Crockett

from DAVY CROCKETT

Words by Tom Blackburn
Music by George Bruns

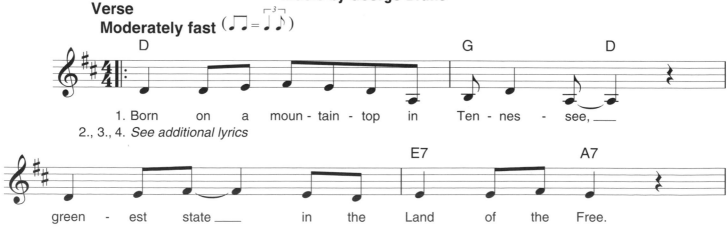

Verse
Moderately fast

1. Born on a moun-tain-top in Ten-nes-see, ___
2., 3., 4. *See additional lyrics*

green-est state ___ in the Land of the Free.

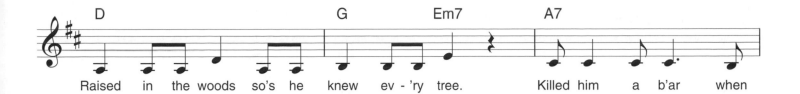

Raised in the woods so's he knew ev-'ry tree. Killed him a b'ar when

he was on-ly three. Da - vy, Da - vy Crock-ett,

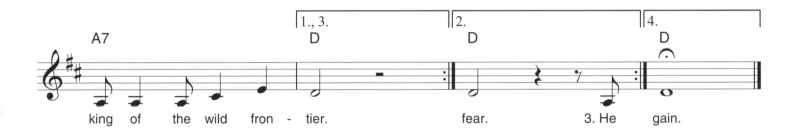

king of the wild fron - tier. fear. 3. He gain.

Additional Lyrics

2. Fought single-handed through the Injun War
   Till the Creeks was whipped and peace was in store.
   And while he was handlin' this risky chore,
   Made himself a legend forevermore.
   Davy, Davy Crockett, the man who don't know fear.

3. He went off to Congress and served a spell,
   Fixin' up the government and laws as well.
   Took over Washington, so we heard tell,
   And patched up the crack in the Liberty Bell.
   Davy, Davy Crockett, seein' his duty clear.

4. When he come home, his politickin' done.
   The western march had just begun.
   So he packed his gear and his trusty gun
   And lit out a grinnin' to follow the sun.
   Davy, Davy Crockett, headin' out west again.

Standard Ukulele

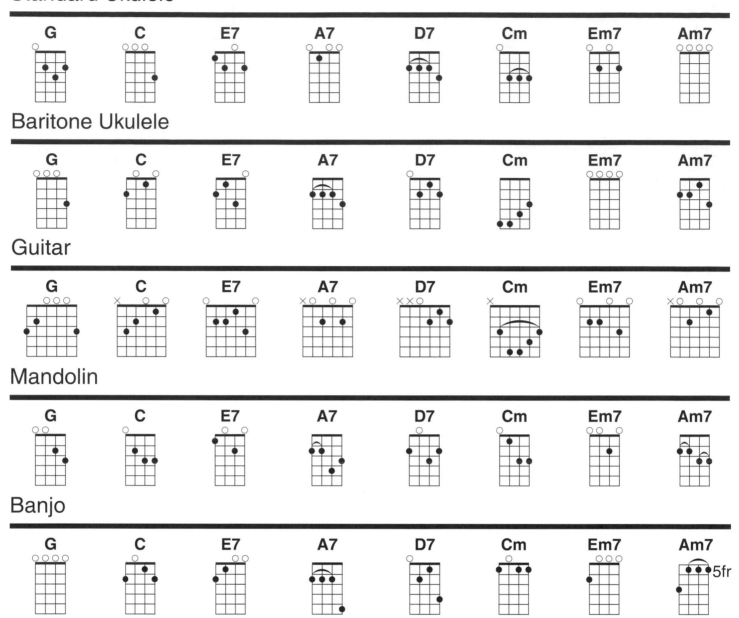

Baritone Ukulele

Guitar

Mandolin

Banjo

The Bare Necessities
from THE JUNGLE BOOK
Words and Music by Terry Gilkyson

1. Look for the bare ne - ces - si - ties, the sim - ple bare ne - ces - si - ties. For - get a - bout your wor - ries and your strife. I mean the

Standard Ukulele

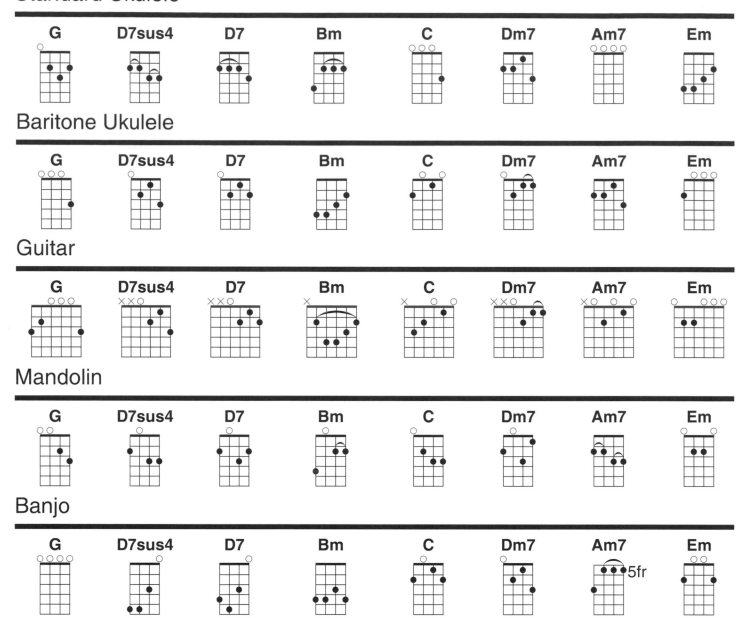

Baritone Ukulele

Guitar

Mandolin

Banjo

Beauty and the Beast

from BEAUTY AND THE BEAST

Music by Alan Menken
Lyrics by Howard Ashman

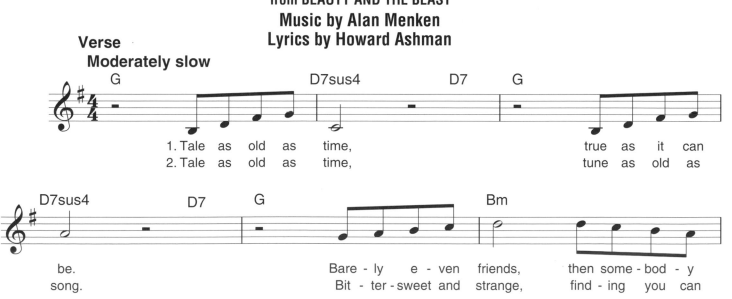

bends un - ex - pect - ed - ly. Just a lit - tle
change, learn - ing you were wrong. Cer - tain as the

change; small, to say the least. Both a lit - tle
sun ris - ing in the east. Tale as old as

scared, nei - ther one pre - pared, Beau - ty and the Beast.
time, song as old as rhyme, Beau - ty and the Beast.

Bridge

Ev - er just the same, ev - er a sur -

prise, ev - er as be - fore, ev - er just as

D.C. al Coda **Coda**

sure as the sun will rise. Tale as old as

time, song as old as rhyme, Beau - ty and the Beast.

Standard Ukulele

Baritone Ukulele

Guitar

Mandolin

Banjo

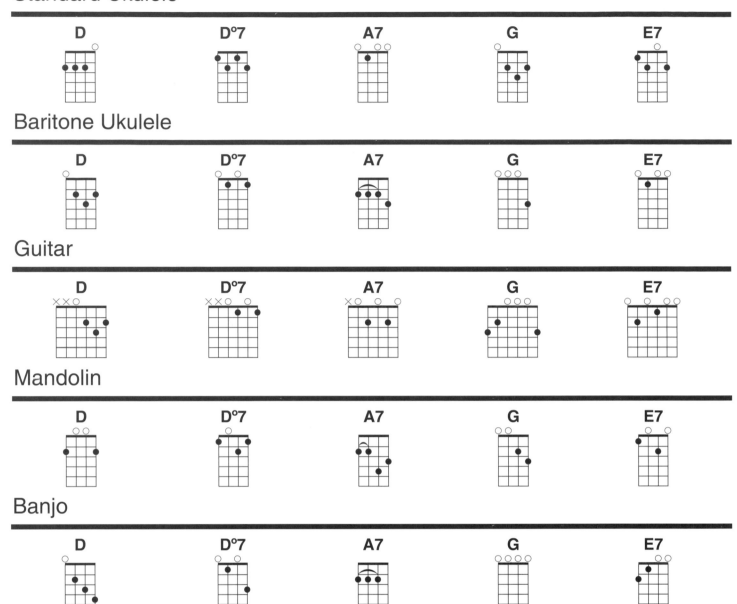

Bibbidi-Bobbidi-Boo
(The Magic Song)
from CINDERELLA
Words by Jerry Livingston
Music by Mack David and Al Hoffman

what have you got? Bib - bi - di - bob - bi - di - boo.   boo.   Now,
lieve it or not. Bib - bi - di - bob - bi - di -

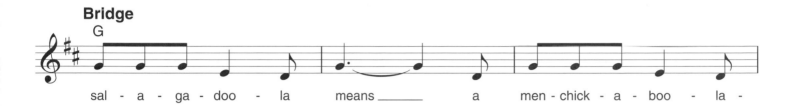

Bridge

sal - a - ga - doo - la   means _____   a   men - chick - a - boo - la -

roo,   but   the   thing - a - ma - bob   that   does   the   job   is

Verse

bib - bi - di - bob - bi - di - boo.   3. Sal - a - ga - doo - la

men - chick - a - boo - la   bib - bi - di - bob - bi - di - boo.

Put 'em to - geth - er   and   what have you got?   Bib - bi - di - bob - bi - di,

bib - bi - di - bob - bi - di,   bib - bi - di - bob - bi - di - boo.

Standard Ukulele

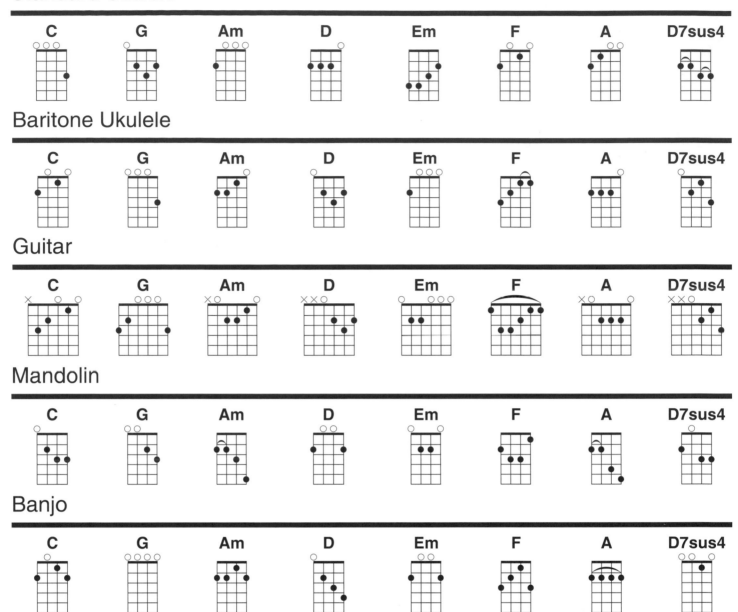

Baritone Ukulele

Guitar

Mandolin

Banjo

Can You Feel the Love Tonight

from THE LION KING
Music by Elton John
Lyrics by Tim Rice

Verse
Moderately slow, in 2

1. There's a calm __ sur - ren - der to the rush __ of day, __
2. There's a time __ for ev - 'ry - one if they on - ly learn __

__ when the heat __ of a roll - ing wind __
__ that the twist - ing ka - lei - do - scope __

can't be turned __ a - way. __   An en - chant - ed mo - ment,
moves us all __ in turn. __   There's a rhyme __ and rea - son

and it sees __ me through. __   It's e - nough __ for this
to the wild __ out - doors __   when the heart __ of this

rest - less war - ri - or just to be __ with you. __ ⎫
star - crossed voy - ag - er beats in time __ with yours. __ ⎬   And

Chorus

can you feel __ the love __ to - night? __   It is where __

__ we are. __   It's e - nough __ for this wide - eyed __

wan - der - er that we got this far. __   And

can you feel __ the love __ to - night, __   how it's laid __

__ to rest? __   It's e - nough __ to make kings __ and __

vag - a - bonds __ be - lieve the ver - y best. __

Standard Ukulele

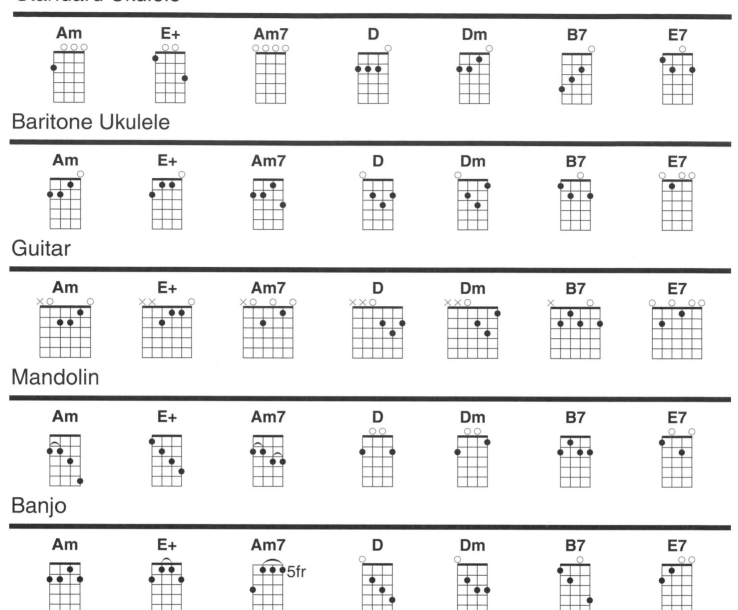

Baritone Ukulele

Guitar

Mandolin

Banjo

Chim Chim Cher-ee
from MARY POPPINS
Words and Music by Richard M. Sherman and Robert B. Sherman

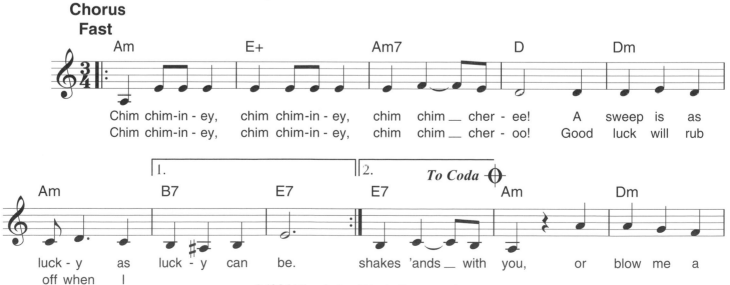

Chorus
Fast

Chim chim-in - ey, chim chim-in - ey, chim chim __ cher - ee! A sweep is as
Chim chim-in - ey, chim chim-in - ey, chim chim __ cher - oo! Good luck will rub

luck - y as luck - y can be.   shakes 'ands __ with you,   or blow me a
off when I

Standard Ukulele

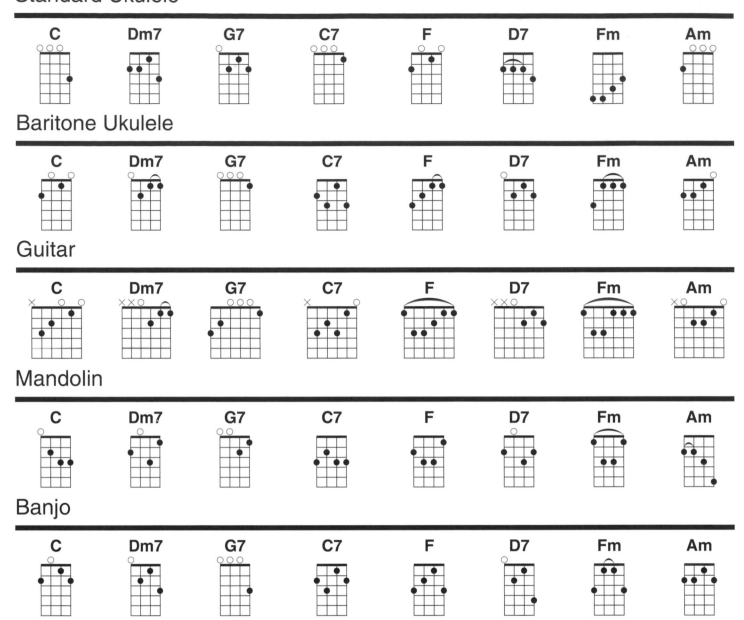

Baritone Ukulele

Guitar

Mandolin

Banjo

Cinderella
from CINDERELLA
Words and Music by Mack David, Al Hoffman and Jerry Livingston

Verse
Moderately slow, in 2

1. Cin - der - el - la, _____ you're as love - ly as your

name. Cin - der - el - la, _____ you're a sun - set _____ in a

frame. Though you're dressed in rags, you wear an

air of queen - ly grace. An - y - one can

see a throne would be your pro - per place. 2. Cin - der -

Verse

el - la, _____ if you give your heart a

chance, it will lead you _____ to the

king - dom of ro - mance. There you'll see your

dreams un - fold, _____ Cin - der - el - la, _____

___ Cin - der - el - la, _____ in the

sweet - est sto - ry ev - er told. _____

Standard Ukulele

Baritone Ukulele

Guitar

Mandolin

Banjo

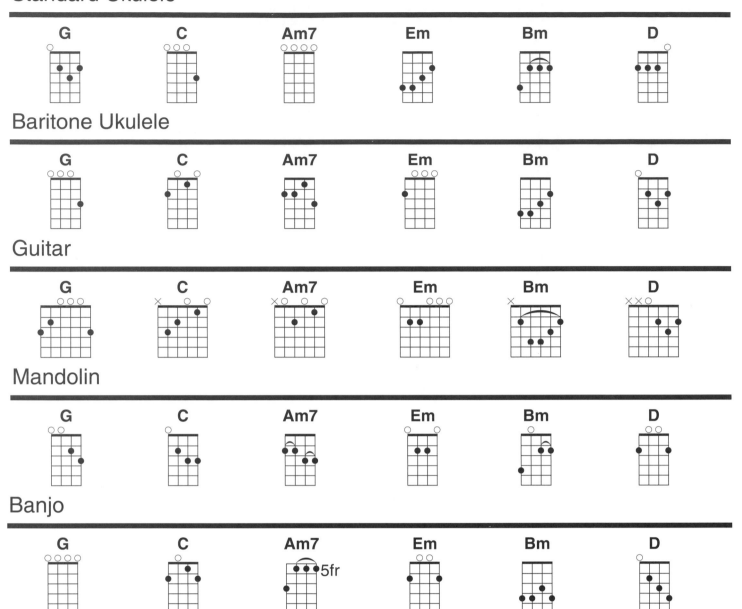

The Climb
from HANNAH MONTANA: THE MOVIE
Words and Music by Jessi Alexander and Jon Mabe

Verse
Moderately

1. I can al - most see it, that dream I'm dream-in'; but
2. The strug-gles I'm fac - ing, the chanc-es I'm tak - ing

there's a voice in - side my head say-ing, "You'll nev - er reach it."
some - times might knock me down, but ___ no, I'm not break - ing.

Chorus

21

Standard Ukulele

Baritone Ukulele

Guitar

Mandolin

Banjo

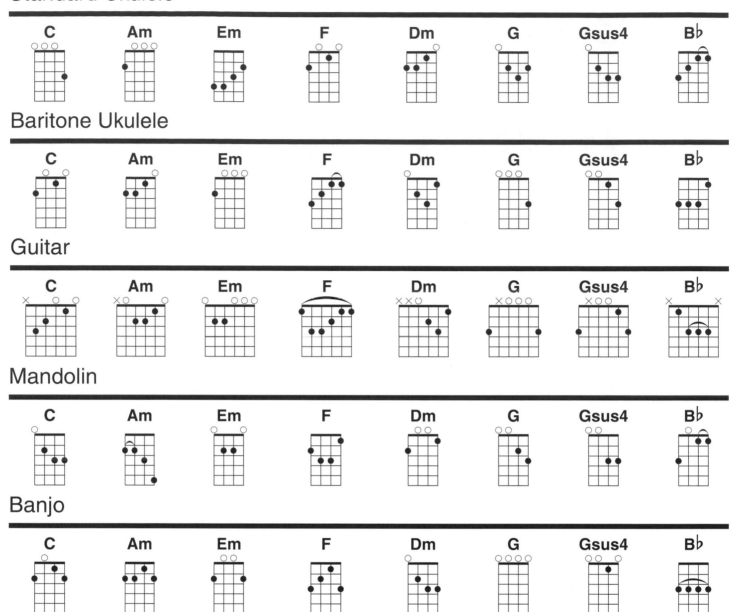

Colors of the Wind
from POCAHONTAS
Music by Alan Menken
Lyrics by Stephen Schwartz

Moderately

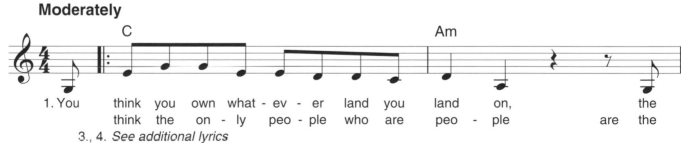

1. You think you own what-ev-er land you land on, the
think the on-ly peo-ple who are peo-ple are the
3., 4. See additional lyrics

earth is just a dead thing you can claim; but I know ev-'ry rock and tree and
peo-ple who look and think like you, but if you walk the foot-steps of a

Additional Lyrics

3. Come run the hidden pine trails of the forest.
   Come taste the sun-sweet berries of the earth.
   Come roll in all the riches all around you,
   And for once never wonder what they're worth.

4. The rainstorm and the river are my brothers.
   The heron and the otter are my friends.
   And we are all connected to each other
   In a circle, in a hoop that never ends.

Standard Ukulele

Baritone Ukulele

Guitar

Mandolin

Banjo

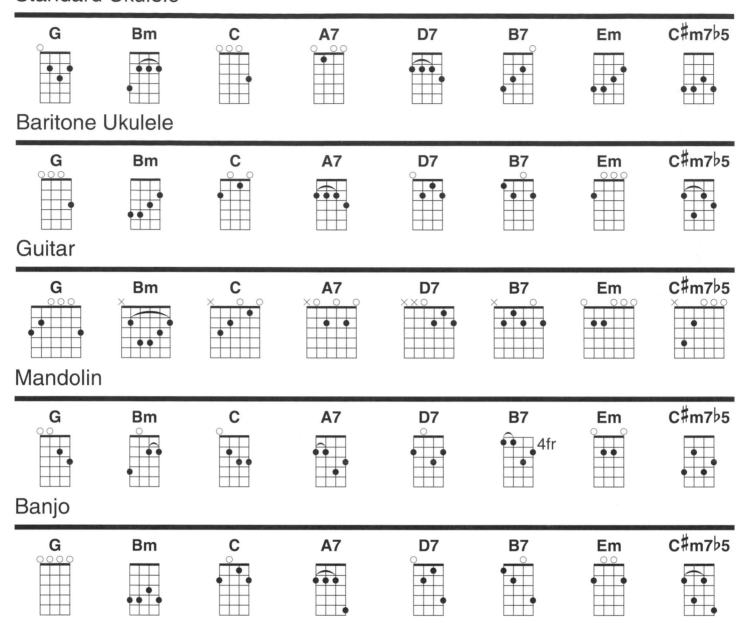

Feed the Birds
(Tuppence a Bag)
from MARY POPPINS
Words and Music by Richard M. Sherman and Robert B. Sherman

Verse
Moderately

1. Feed _____ the birds, tup-pence _____ a bag, tup-pence, _____

tup-pence, _____ tup-pence _____ a bag. "Feed _____ the birds,"

that's what ___ she cries while o - ver - head her birds fill the

Bridge

skies.   All a - round the ca - the - dral ___ the saints and a -

pos - tles ___ look down as she sells her wares. _____   Al -

though you can't see it, ___ you know they are smil - ing ___ each

Verse

time some - one shows that he cares. _____   2. Though ___ her

words are sim - ple ___ and few, lis - ten, ___ lis - ten, ___ she's

call - ing to you.   Feed ___ the birds, tup - pence ___ a

bag,   tup - pence, ___ tup - pence, ___ tup - pence a bag.

Standard Ukulele

Baritone Ukulele

Guitar

Mandolin

Banjo

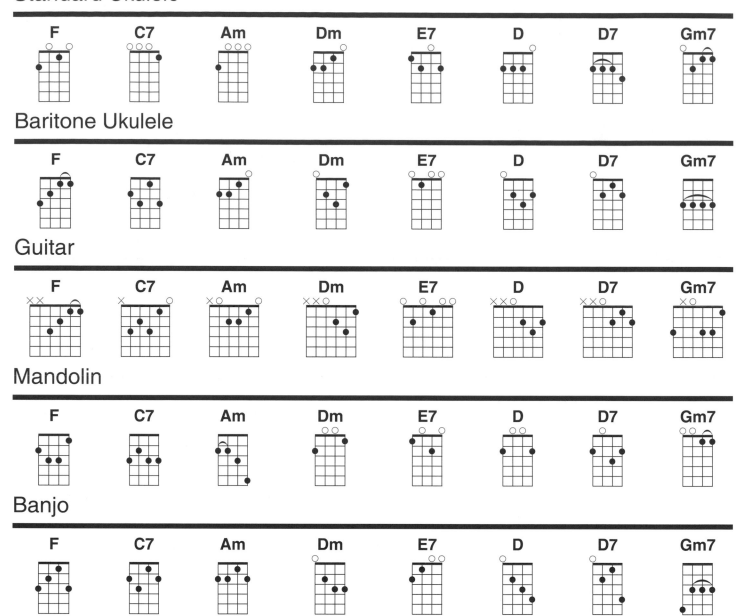

Give a Little Whistle

from PINOCCHIO
Words by Ned Washington
Music by Leigh Harline

Verse
Moderately, in 2

1. When you get in trou - ble and you don't know right from

wrong, give a lit - tle whis - tle! *Whistle:* _____ Give a lit - tle

Standard Ukulele

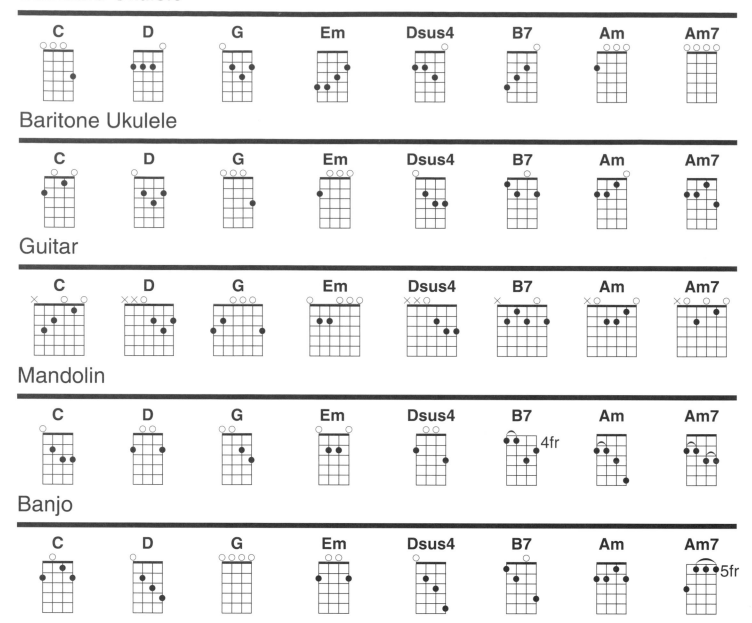

Baritone Ukulele

Guitar

Mandolin

Banjo

Go the Distance

from HERCULES

Music by Alan Menken
Lyrics by David Zippel

Standard Ukulele

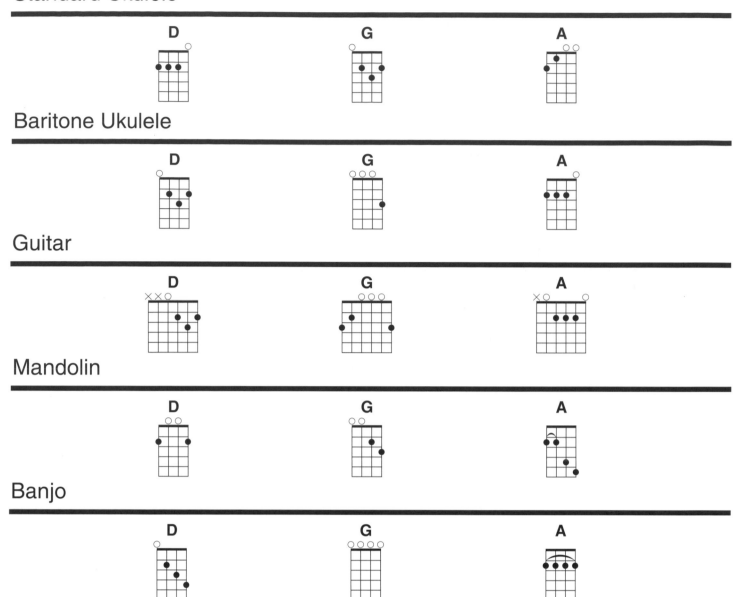

Baritone Ukulele

Guitar

Mandolin

Banjo

Hawaiian Roller Coaster Ride

from LILO & STITCH

Words and Music by Alan Silvestri and Mark Keali'i Ho'omalu

1., 3. There's no ___ place I'd rath-er be ___ than on my surf-board out at sea,
2. There's no ___ place I'd rath-er be ___ than on the sea-shore dry, wet, free.

lin-ger-ing ___ in the o-cean blue. ___ And if I had one wish come true, I'd
On gold-en sand is where I'd lay, and if I on-ly had my way I'd

Standard Ukulele

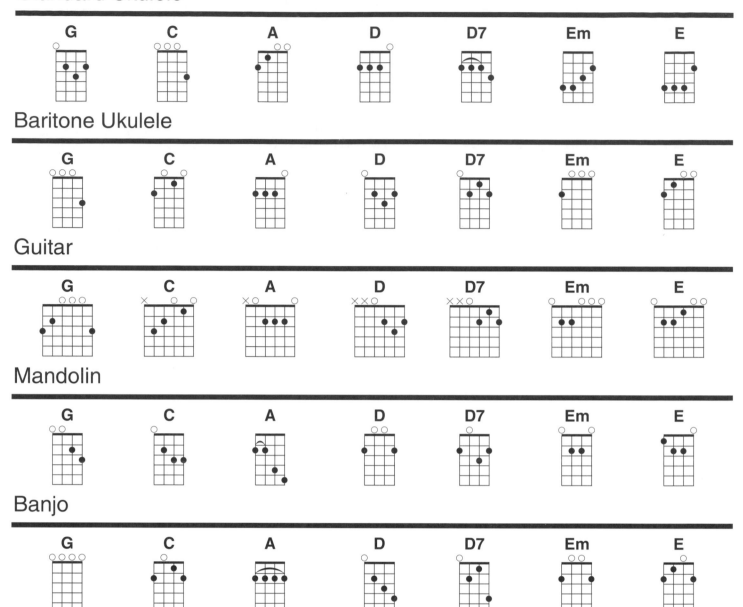

Baritone Ukulele

Guitar

Mandolin

Banjo

Heigh-Ho

The Dwarfs' Marching Song from SNOW WHITE AND THE SEVEN DWARFS

Words by Larry Morey
Music by Frank Churchill

𝄋 Chorus
Moderate March, in 2

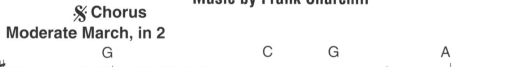

"Heigh - ho, heigh - ho," it's home from work we

go. *Whistle:* "Heigh - ho, heigh -

Standard Ukulele

Baritone Ukulele

Guitar

Mandolin

Banjo

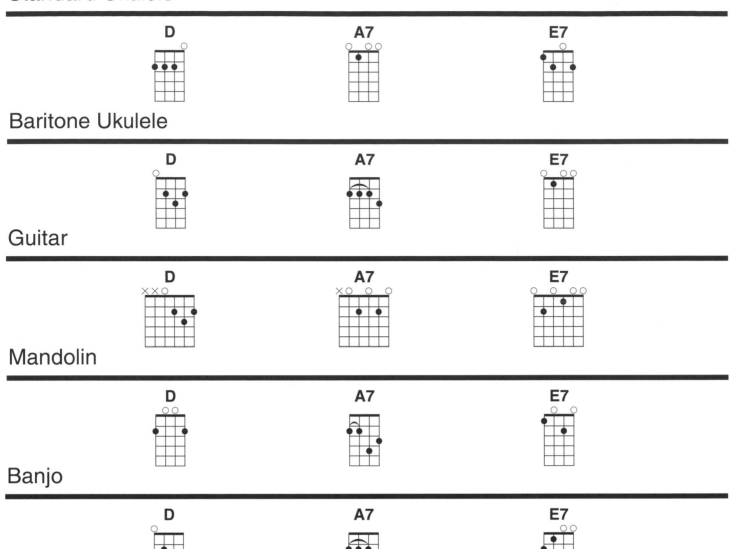

Hi-Diddle-Dee-Dee
(An Actor's Life for Me)
from PINOCCHIO

Words by Ned Washington
Music by Leigh Harline

Standard Ukulele

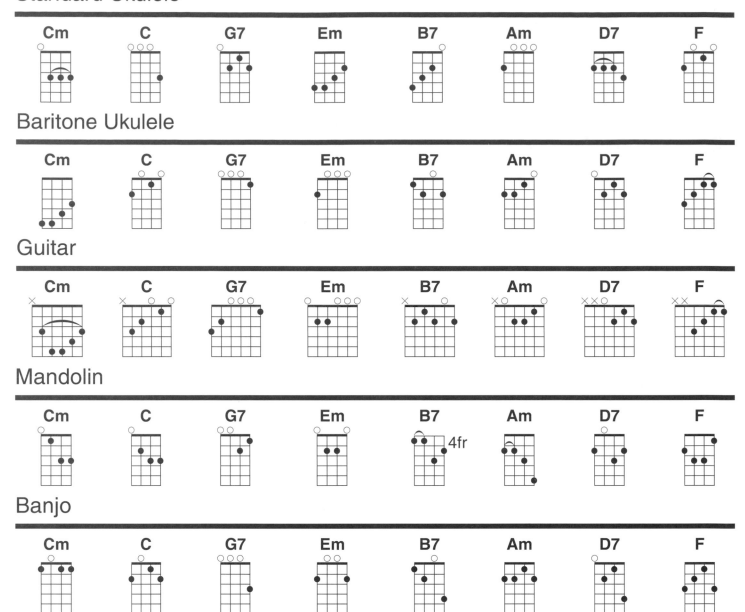

Baritone Ukulele

Guitar

Mandolin

Banjo

I'm Late
from ALICE IN WONDERLAND

Words by Bob Hilliard
Music by Sammy Fain

Moderately fast, in 2

Cm

I'm late, I'm late for a ver-y im-por-tant

C   G7

date. No time to say hel-lo, good-bye; I'm

late, I'm late, I'm late, I'm late. And when I

wave, I lose the time I save. My fuz - zy ears and

whis - kers took me too much time to shave. I

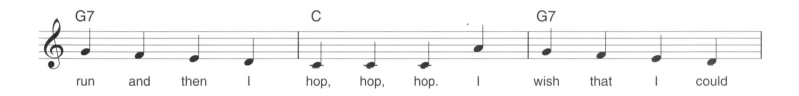

run and then I hop, hop, hop. I wish that I could

fly. There's dan - ger if I dare to stop and

here's the rea - son why: you see, I'm o - ver -

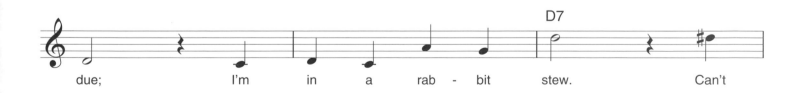

due; I'm in a rab - bit stew. Can't

e - ven say good - bye, hel - lo; I'm late, I'm late, I'm late.

Standard Ukulele

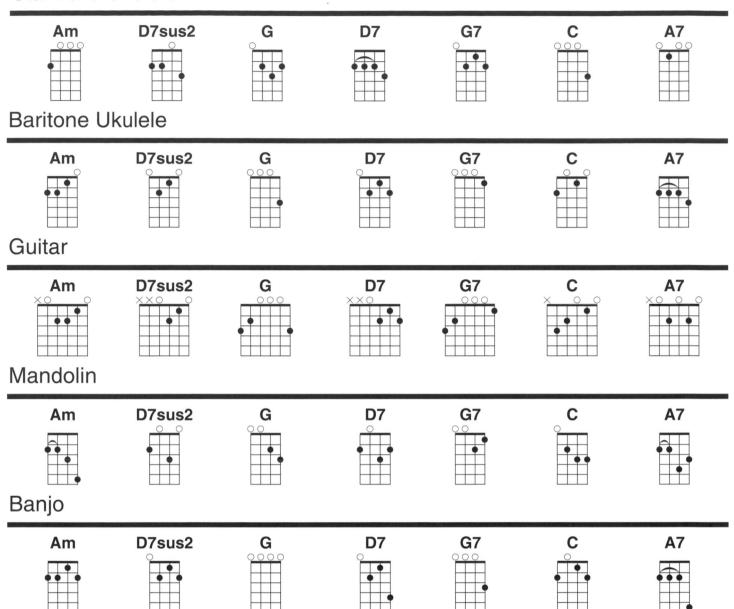

Baritone Ukulele

Guitar

Mandolin

Banjo

I'm Wishing

from SNOW WHITE AND THE SEVEN DWARFS
Words by Larry Morey
Music by Frank Churchill

Intro
Moderately, in 2

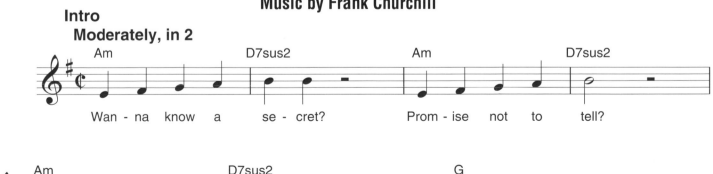

Wan - na know a se - cret? Prom - ise not to tell?

We are stand - ing by a wish - ing well.

Standard Ukulele

Baritone Ukulele

Guitar

Mandolin

Banjo

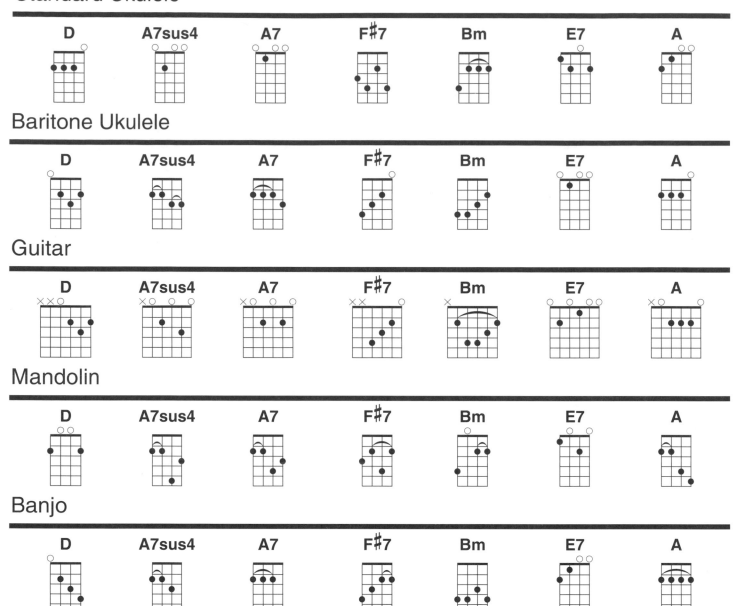

I've Got No Strings

from PINOCCHIO
Words by Ned Washington
Music by Leigh Harline

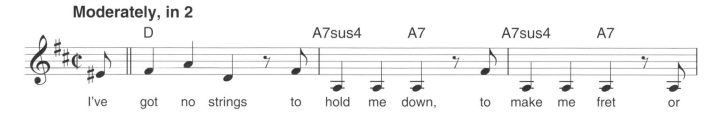

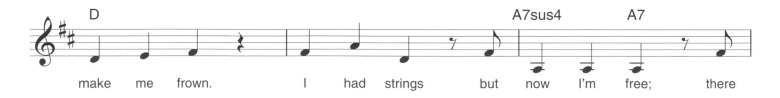

are no strings on me. Hi - ho the

mer - ri - o, that's the on - ly way to be.

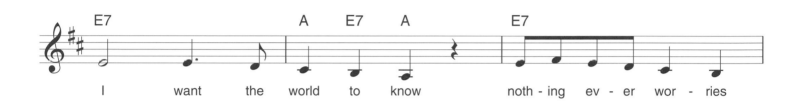

I want the world to know noth - ing ev - er wor - ries

Outro-Chorus

me. I've got no strings so I have fun; I'm

not tied up to an - y - one. They've got strings but

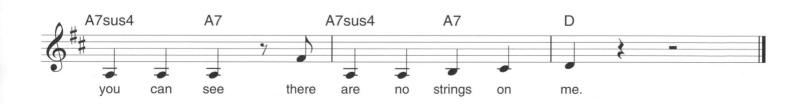

you can see there are no strings on me.

Standard Ukulele

Baritone Ukulele

Guitar

Mandolin

Banjo

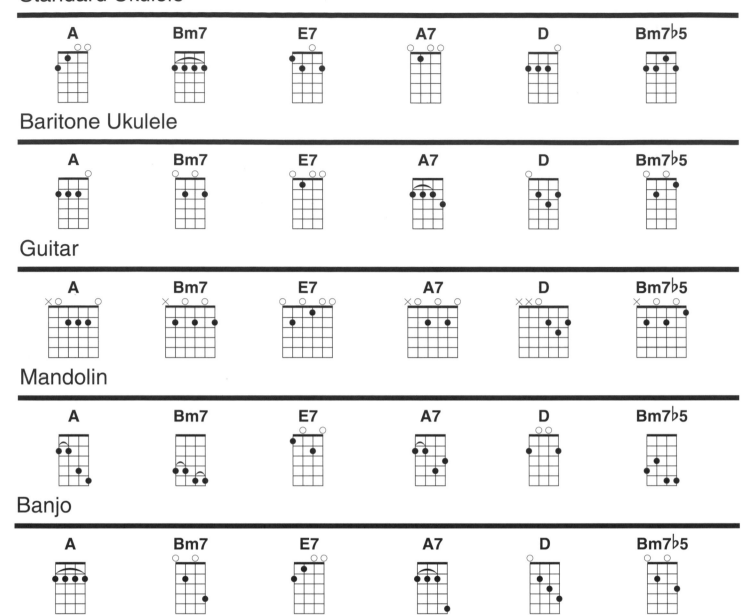

It's a Small World
from Disney Parks' "it's a small world" attraction

Words and Music by Richard M. Sherman and Robert B. Sherman

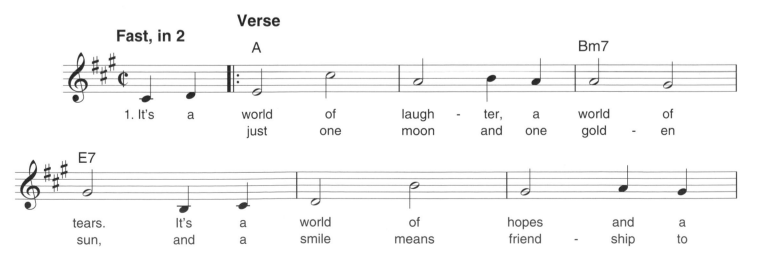

1. It's a world of laugh - ter, a world of tears. It's a world of hopes and a

just one moon and one gold - en sun, and a smile means friend - ship to

Standard Ukulele

Baritone Ukulele

Guitar

Mandolin

Banjo

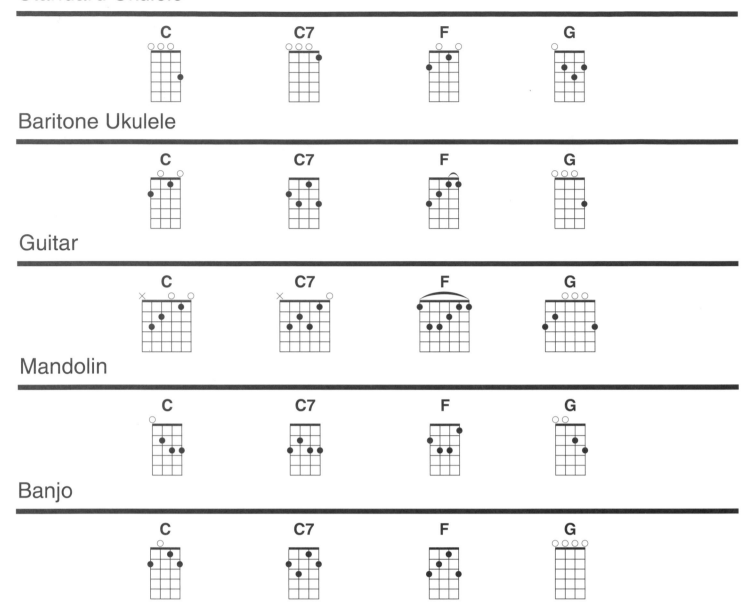

Kiss the Girl

from THE LITTLE MERMAID

Music by Alan Menken
Lyrics by Howard Ashman

Verse
Moderately fast Calypso feel

1. There you see ___ her sit - ting there a - cross the way. ___

___ She don't got a lot to say, ___ but there's some - thing a -

bout her. ___ And you don't ___ know why, ___ but you're dy -

Verse

- ing to try. You wan - na kiss the girl.

2. Yes, you want ___
3. Now's your mo -

___ her.

___ - ment, Look at her; you know you do. ___

float - ing in a blue la - goon. ___

Pos - si - ble she wants you too. ___ There is one ___ way to ask her. ___

Boy, you bet - ter do it soon; ___ no time ___ will be bet - ter. ___

It don't take a word, ___ not a sin - gle word; ___ go on and

She don't say a word ___ and she won't ___ say a word un - til you

𝄋 Chorus

kiss the girl.
kiss the girl.

Sha, la, la, la, la, la,
Sha, la, la, la, la, la,
Sha, la, la, la, la, la,

my oh my. ___ Look like the boy too shy; ___ ain't gon - na kiss the girl.

don't be scared. ___ You got the mood pre - pared; ___ go on and kiss the girl.

float a - long ___ and lis - ten to the song; ___ the song say, "Kiss the girl."

To Coda ⊕

Sha, la, la, la, la, la, ain't that sad. ___ ain't it a shame, too bad. ___ He gon - na

Sha, la, la, la, la, la, don't stop now. ___ Don't try to hide it how ___ you wan - na

Sha, la, la, la, la, the mu - sic play. ___ Do what the mu - sic say. ___ You got - ta

1.

D.S. al Coda   ⊕ *Coda*

2.

miss the girl. ___

kiss the girl.

kiss the girl.

Standard Ukulele

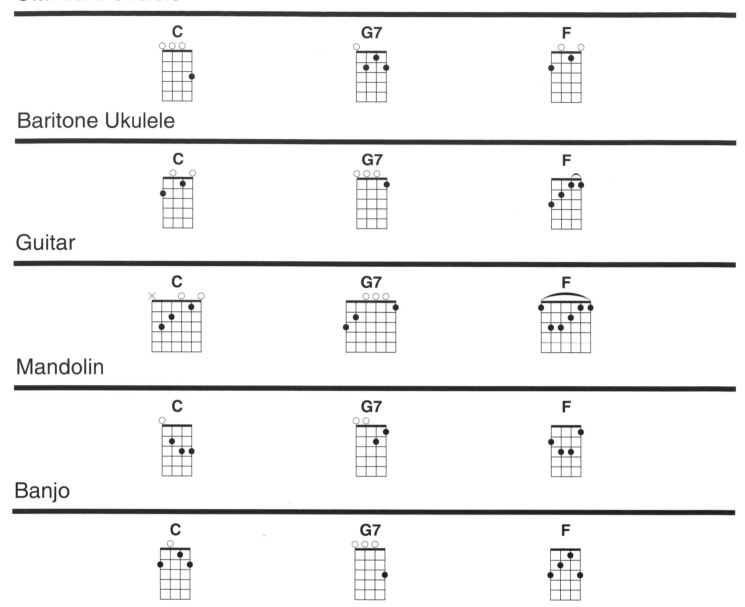

Baritone Ukulele

Guitar

Mandolin

Banjo

Lava

from LAVA

Music and Lyrics by James Ford Murphy

Verse
Moderately fast

1. A long, long time a-go ___ there was a vol-ca-no ___
2.-12. *See additional lyrics*

liv-ing all a - lone ___ in the mid-dle of ___ the sea.

*Play 3 times

*On 1st D.C. play 4 times (verses 4-7);
on 2nd D.C. play 3 times (verses 8-10);
on 3rd D.C. play 2 times (verses 11-12)

Additional Lyrics

2. He sat high above his bay watching all the couples play
   And wishing that he had someone too.

3. And from his lava came this song of hope
   That he sang out loud every day for years and years.

4. Years of singing all alone turned his lava into stone
   Until he was on the brink of extinction.

5. But little did he know that living in the sea below
   Another volcano was listening to his song.

6. Everyday she heard his tune, her lava grew and grew
   Because she believed his song was meant for her.

7. Now she was so ready to meet him above the sea
   As he sang his song of hope for the last time.

8. Rising from the sea below stood a lovely volcano
   Looking all around but she could not see him.

9. He tried to sing to let her know that she was not there alone
   But with no lava, his song was all gone.

10. He filled the sea with his tears and watched his dreams disappear
    As she remembered what his song meant to her.

11. Oh, they were so happy to finally meet above the sea;
    All together now their lava grew and grew.

12. No longer are they all alone with aloha as their new home
    And when you visit them, this is what they sing:

Standard Ukulele

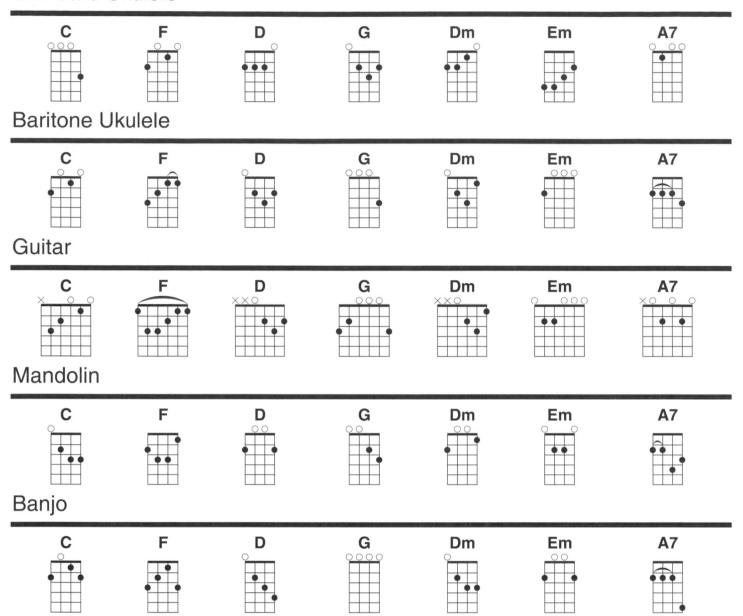

Baritone Ukulele

Guitar

Mandolin

Banjo

Lavender Blue
(Dilly Dilly)
from SO DEAR TO MY HEART
Words by Larry Morey
Music by Eliot Daniel

1. Lav - en - der blue, dil - ly, dil - ly, lav - en - der

green. If I were king, dil - ly, dil - ly,

Standard Ukulele

Baritone Ukulele

Guitar

Mandolin

Banjo

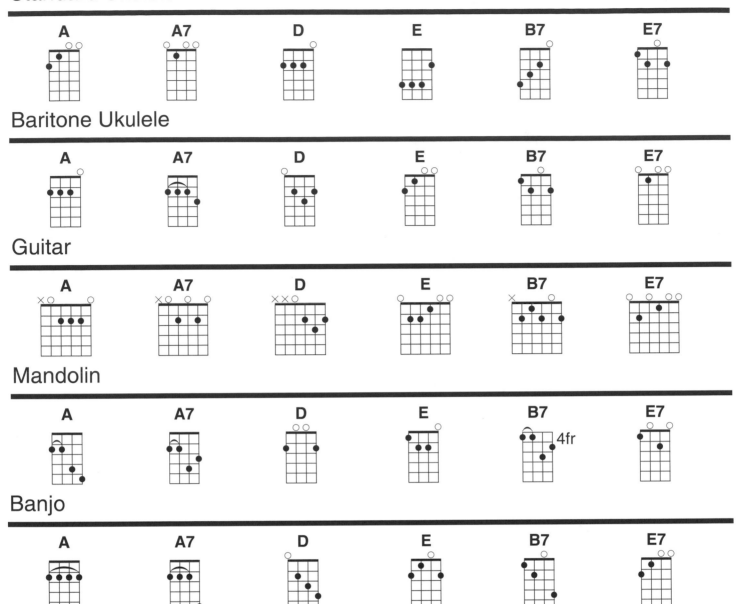

Let's Get Together

from THE PARENT TRAP

Words and Music by Richard M. Sherman and Robert B. Sherman

Verse
Moderately fast

1. Let's get to-geth-er, yay, yay, yay. — Why don't you and I com-bi-
2. Let's get to-geth-er, yay, yay, yay. — Think of all that we could sha-

- ine? Let's get to-geth-er, what do you say? —
- are. Let's get to-geth-er ev-'ry day, —

Standard Ukulele

Baritone Ukulele

Guitar

Mandolin

Banjo

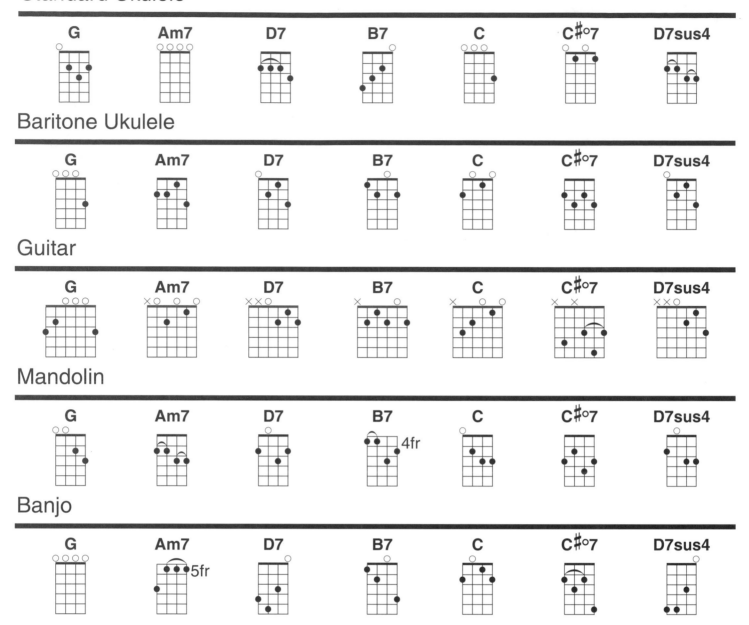

Let's Go Fly a Kite
from MARY POPPINS
Words and Music by Richard M. Sherman and Robert B. Sherman

Verse
Moderately, in 1

1. With tup-pence for pa-per and strings, you can have your own set of wings.

send it fly-ing up there, all at once you're light-er than air. With your You can

feet on the ground you're a bird ____ in flight
dance on the breeze o - ver hous - es and trees } with your

fist hold - ing tight to the string of your

Chorus

kite. Oh. ____ Let's go

fly a kite up to the high - est

height. Let's go fly a kite and send

it soar - ing up through the

at - mos - phere, up where the air is clear.

1.
Oh, let's go ____ fly a kite.

2.
2. When you kite. ____

Standard Ukulele

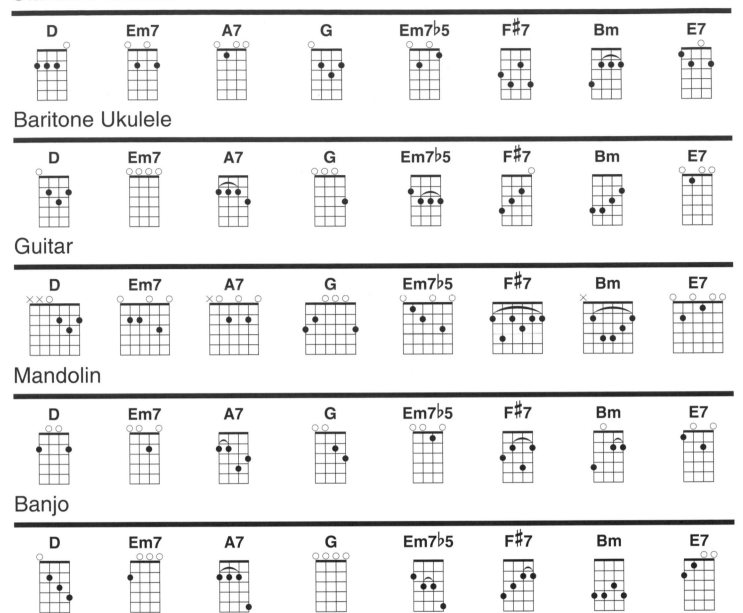

Baritone Ukulele

Guitar

Mandolin

Banjo

The Lord Is Good to Me
from MELODY TIME
Words and Music by Kim Gannon and Walter Kent

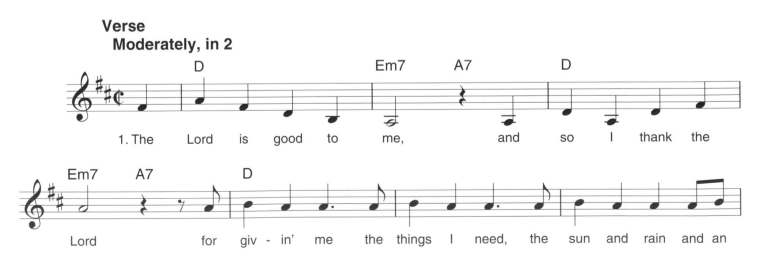

Verse
Moderately, in 2

1. The Lord is good to me, and so I thank the
Lord for giv - in' me the things I need, the sun and rain and an

ap - ple seed. Yes, He's been good to me.

Verse

2. I owe the Lord so much for ev - 'ry - thing I

see. I'm cer - tain if it weren't for Him, there'd be no ap - ples

on this limb. Yes, He's been good to me. Oh,

Bridge

here am I 'neath a blue, blue sky a do - in' as I please,

sing - in' with my feath - ered friends, hum - min' with the bees. 3. I

Verse

wake up ev - 'ry day as hap - py as can be be -

cause I know that with His care, my ap - ple trees, they will

still be there. Oh, the Lord is good to me.

Standard Ukulele

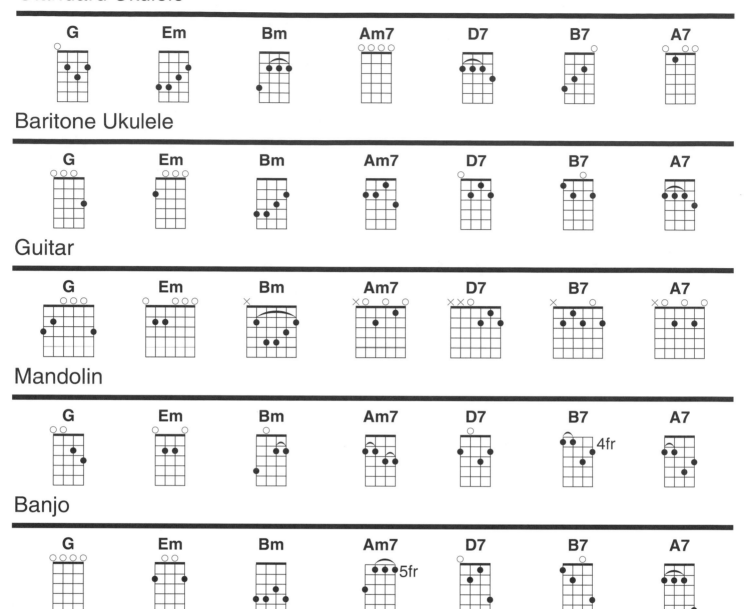

Baritone Ukulele

Guitar

Mandolin

Banjo

Love Is a Song

from BAMBI
Words by Larry Morey
Music by Frank Churchill

Verse
Moderately slow, in 2

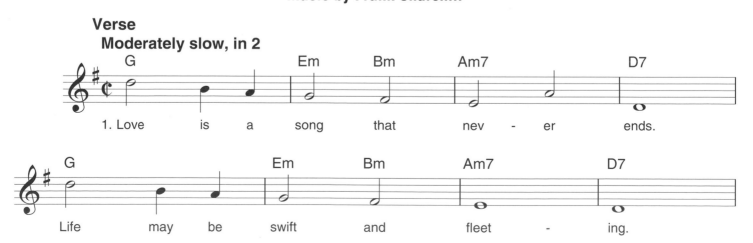

1. Love is a song that nev - er ends.

Life may be swift and fleet - ing.

Hope may die, yet love's beau - ti - ful mu - sic

comes each day like the dawn. _____

Verse

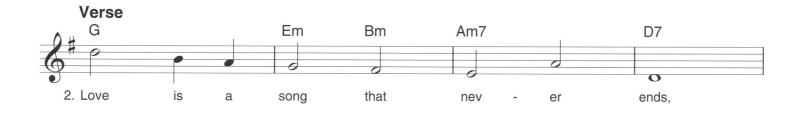

2. Love is a song that nev - er ends,

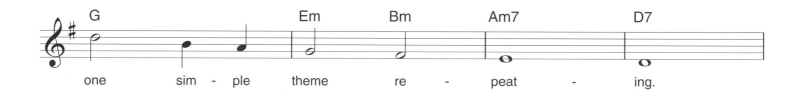

one sim - ple theme re - peat - ing.

Like the voice of a heav - en - ly choir, _____

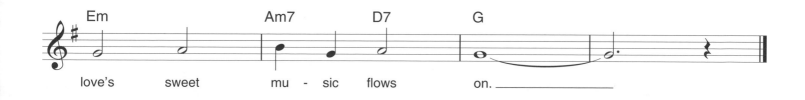

love's sweet mu - sic flows on. _____

Standard Ukulele

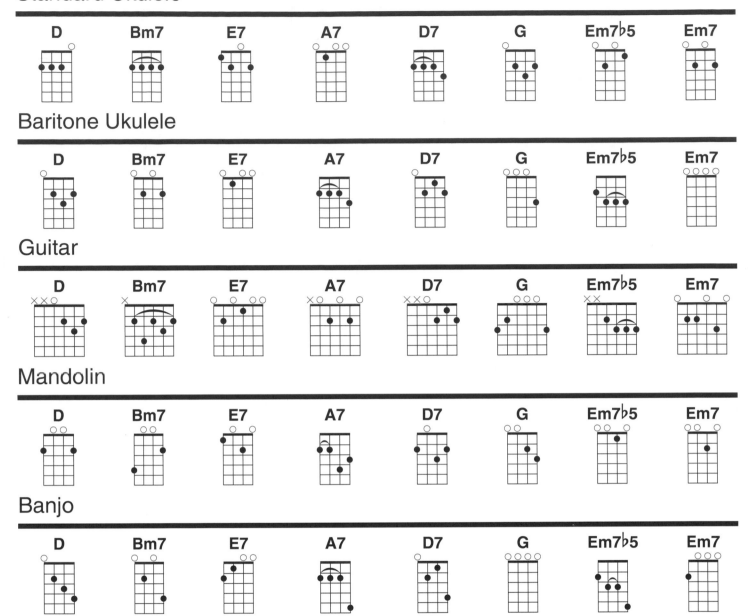

Baritone Ukulele

Guitar

Mandolin

Banjo

Mickey Mouse March

from THE MICKEY MOUSE CLUB

Words and Music by Jimmie Dodd

Standard Ukulele

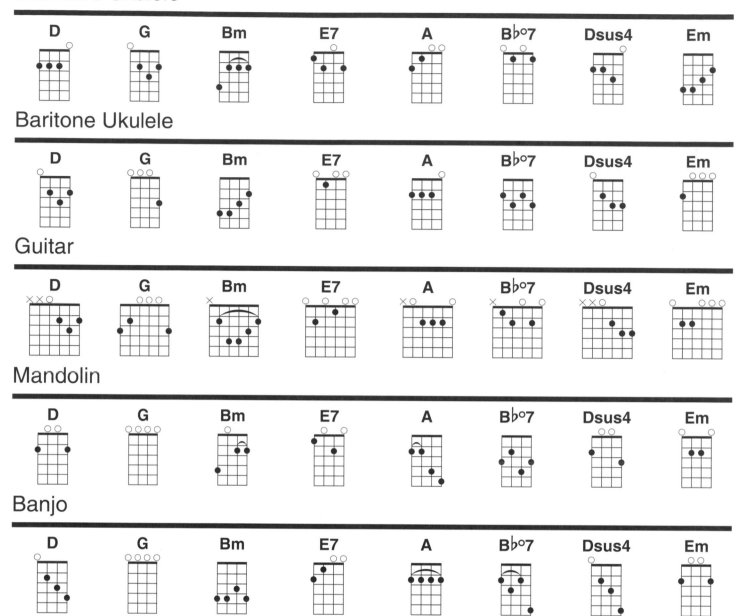

Baritone Ukulele

Guitar

Mandolin

Banjo

Never Smile at a Crocodile

from PETER PAN
Words by Jack Lawrence
Music by Frank Churchill

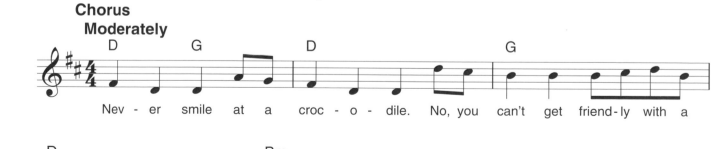

Chorus
Moderately

Nev - er smile at a croc - o - dile. No, you can't get friend-ly with a

croc - o - dile. Don't be tak - en in by his wel - come grin; he's im -

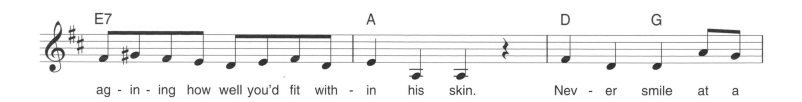

ag - in - ing how well you'd fit with - in his skin. Nev - er smile at a

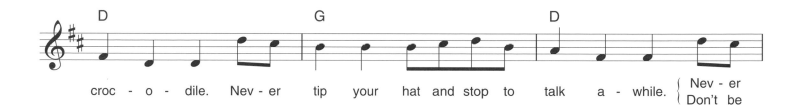

croc - o - dile. Nev - er tip your hat and stop to talk a - while. { Nev - er
Don't be

run, walk a - way. Say "good - night," not "good day." } Clear the
rude, nev - er mock. Throw a kiss, not a rock.

Bridge

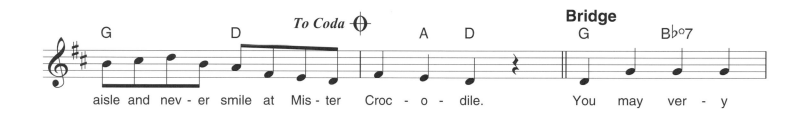

aisle and nev - er smile at Mis - ter Croc - o - dile. You may ver - y

well be well - bred, lots of et - i - quette in your head,

but there's al - ways some spe - cial case, time or place to for - get et - i -

D.C. al Coda   Coda

quette.   Croc - o - dile.

Standard Ukulele

Baritone Ukulele

Guitar

Mandolin

Banjo

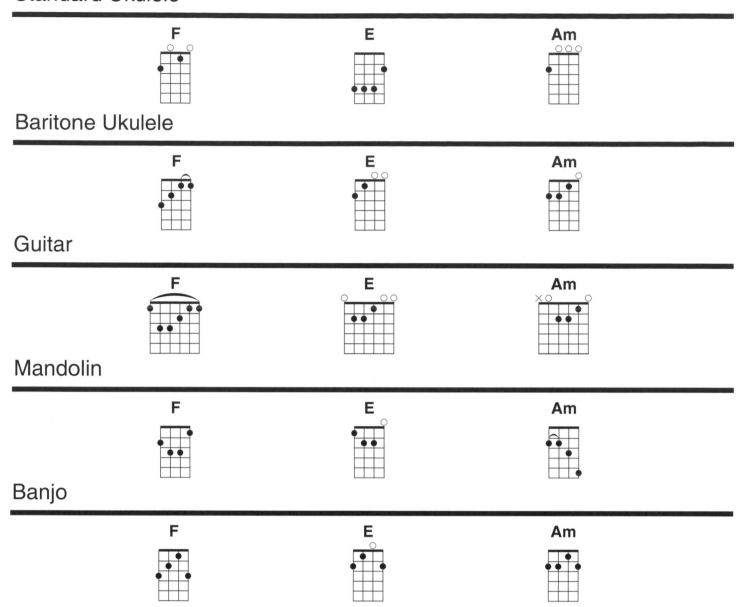

Nobody Like U

from TURNING RED
Music and Lyrics by Billie Eilish and Finneas O'Connell

1. I've nev-er met no-bod-y ___ like ___ you. Had friends and I've had

bud-dies, ___ it's ___ true. ___ But they don't turn my tum-my _____ the way ___

Standard Ukulele

Baritone Ukulele

Guitar

Mandolin

Banjo

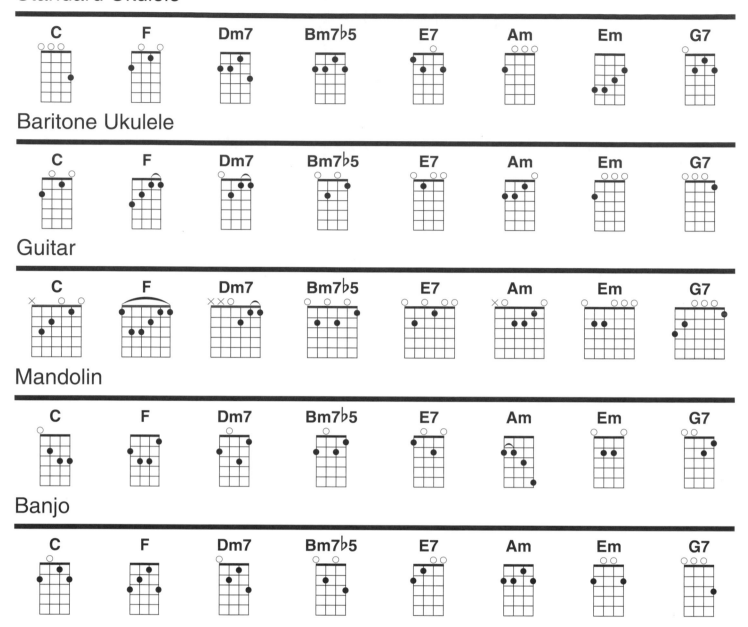

Oh, What a Merry Christmas Day

from MICKEY'S CHRISTMAS CAROL

Words and Music by Irwin Kostal and Frederick Searles

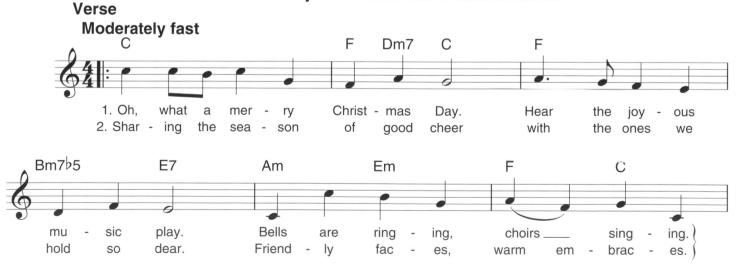

Verse
Moderately fast

1. Oh, what a mer - ry Christ - mas Day. Hear the joy - ous
2. Shar - ing the sea - son of good cheer with the ones we

mu - sic play. Bells are ring - ing, choirs ___ sing - ing.
hold so dear. Friend - ly fac - es, warm em - brac - es.

Standard Ukulele

Baritone Ukulele

Guitar

Mandolin

Banjo

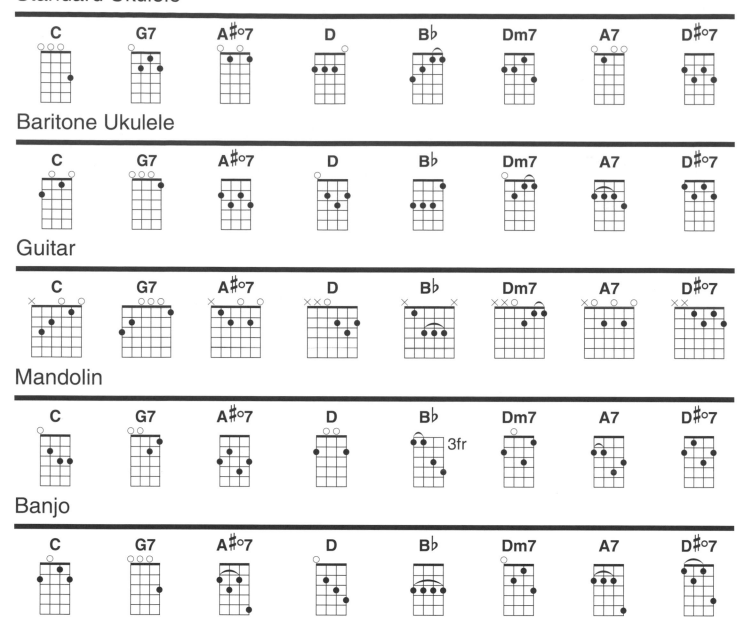

Once Upon a Dream

from SLEEPING BEAUTY
Words and Music by Sammy Fain and Jack Lawrence
Adapted from a theme by Tchaikovsky

I know you; the gleam in your

eyes is so fa - mil - iar a gleam. Yet I

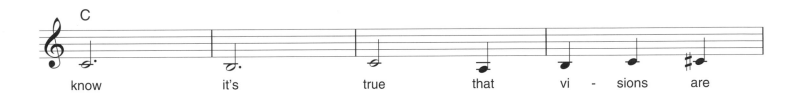

know it's true that vi - sions are

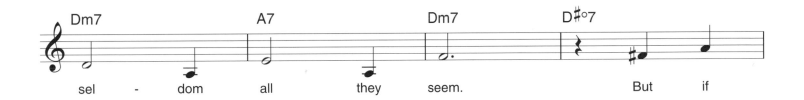

sel - dom all they seem. But if

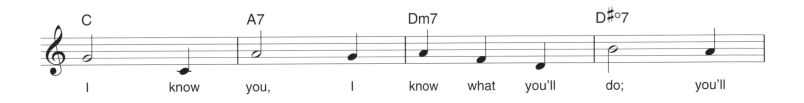

I know you, I know what you'll do; you'll

love me at once the way you did once up -

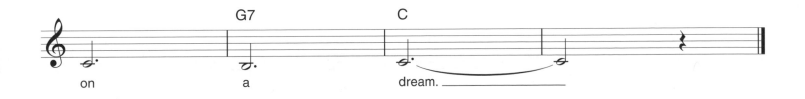

on a dream. _____

Standard Ukulele

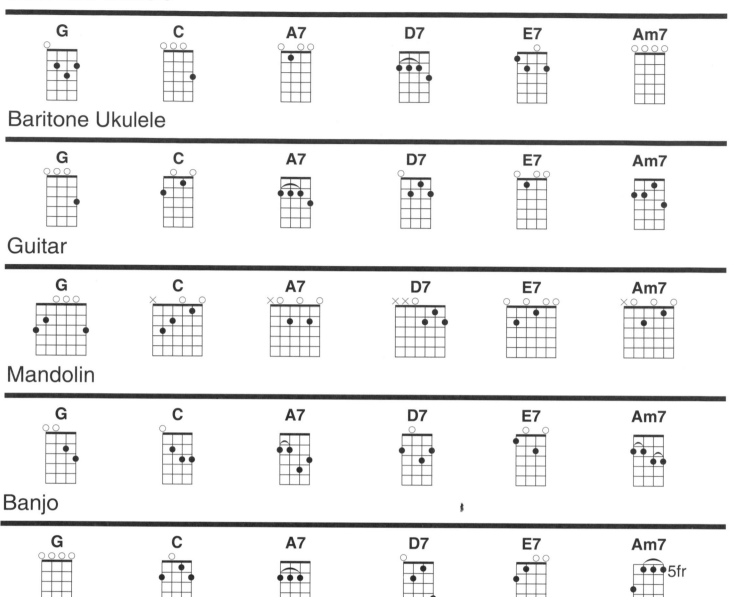

Baritone Ukulele

Guitar

Mandolin

Banjo

A Pirate's Life

from PETER PAN

Words by Ed Penner

Music by Oliver Wallace

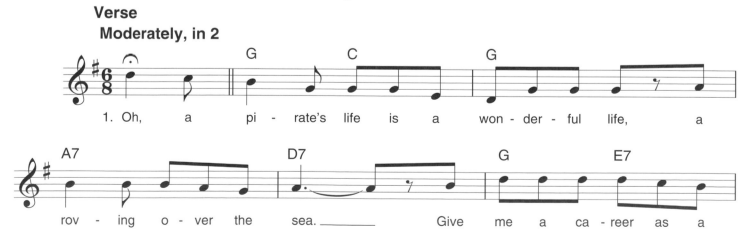

Verse

Moderately, in 2

1. Oh, a pi - rate's life is a won - der - ful life, a

rov - ing o - ver the sea. ___ Give me a ca - reer as a

Buc - ca - neer; it's the life of a pi - rate for me, oh, the

life of a pi - rate for me! _____ 2. Oh, a

Verse

pi - rate's life is a won - der - ful life; they nev - er bur - y your

bones, _____ for when it's all o - ver a jol - ly sea rov - er drops

in on his friend, Da - vy Jones, oh, his ver - y good friend, Da - vy

Verse

Jones. _____ 3. Oh, a pi - rate's life is a

won - der - ful life; you'll find ad - ven - ture and sport. _____ But

live ev - 'ry min - ute for all that is in it; the life of a pi - rate is

short, oh, the life of a pi - rate is short! _____

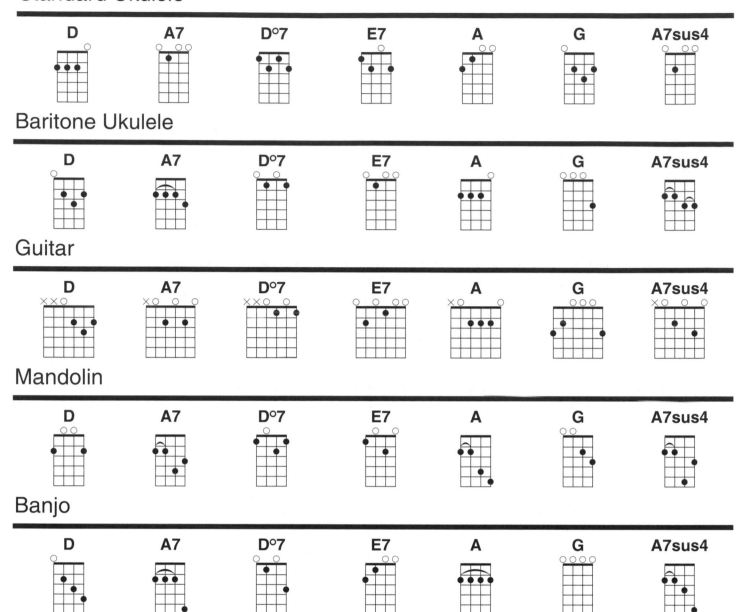

Pollyanna Song

from POLLYANNA

Words by David Swift
Music by Paul Smith

What it is I real-ly think, I think that spring has sprang. I woke up feel-ing tick-led pink, and

Chorus

this is what I sang:

I'm as hap - py

as a lit - tle clam; __ I yam, __ I yam, __ I yam in love.

Just with noth - in' in par - tic - u - lar; __ I yar, __ I yar, __

Bridge

I yar in love. Gra - cious good - ness, dear - ie me, my

saint - ed aunt a - bove. __ Bless my heart, for pit - y's sake, I'm

Outro

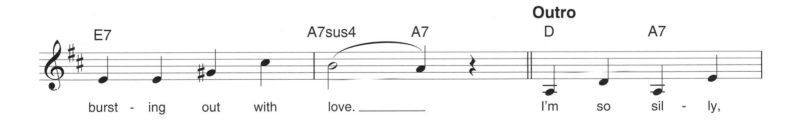

burst - ing out with love. _____ I'm so sil - ly,

tell you why it is: __ I yizz, __ I yizz __ in love with ev - 'ry - one.

Standard Ukulele

Baritone Ukulele

Guitar

Mandolin

Banjo

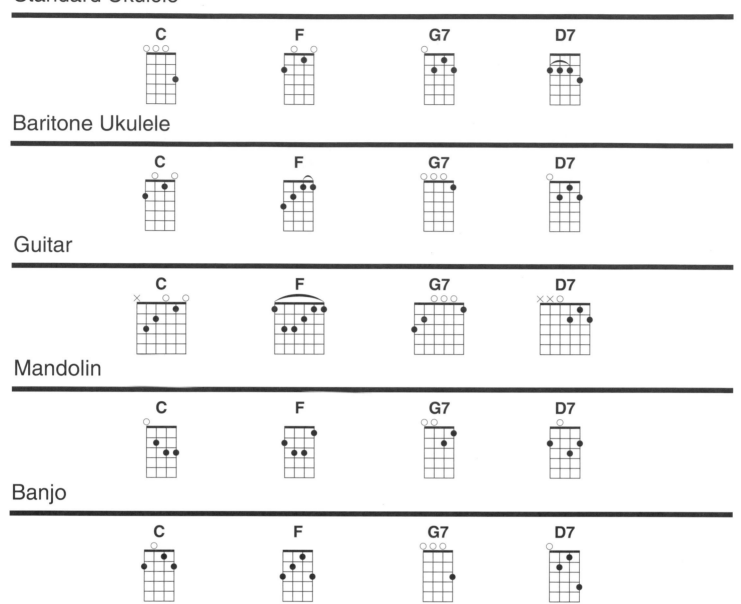

Riddle De Diddle De Day

from THE STORY OF ROBIN HOOD AND HIS MERRY MEN

Words and Music by Edward Pola and George Wyle

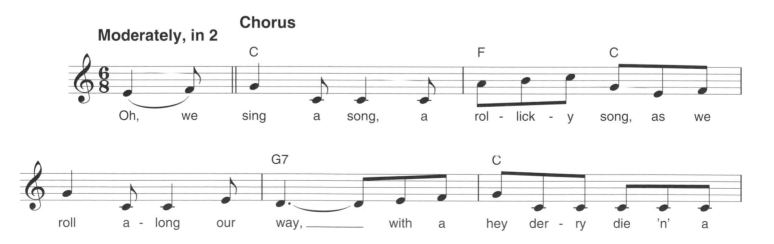

der - ry die do 'n' a rid - dle de did - dle de day. _____ 1. A

Verse

ver - y mer - ry band are we, as we are Rob - in Hood's
all wear coats of lin - coln green, our bows are strong ___ and
one thing you may all be sure, we'll fight un - til _____ we

men. _____ Our like you are not like to see in
stout. _____ If an - y - one is bad or mean, we'll
win. _____ We rob the rich to help the poor, and

Chorus

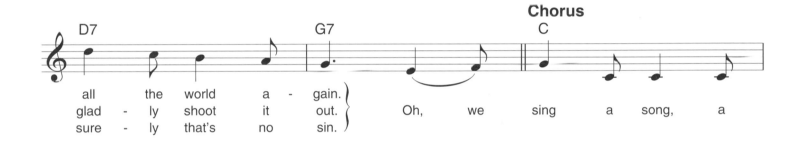

all the world a - gain. } Oh, we sing a song, a
glad - ly shoot it out. }
sure - ly that's no sin. }

rol - lick - y song, as we roll a - long our way, _____ with a

hey der - ry die 'n' a der - ry die do 'n' a

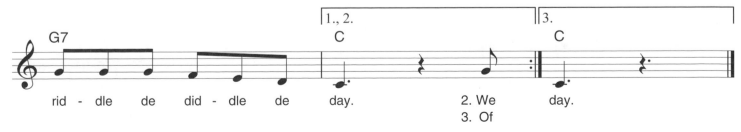

rid - dle de did - dle de day. 2. We day.
3. Of

Standard Ukulele

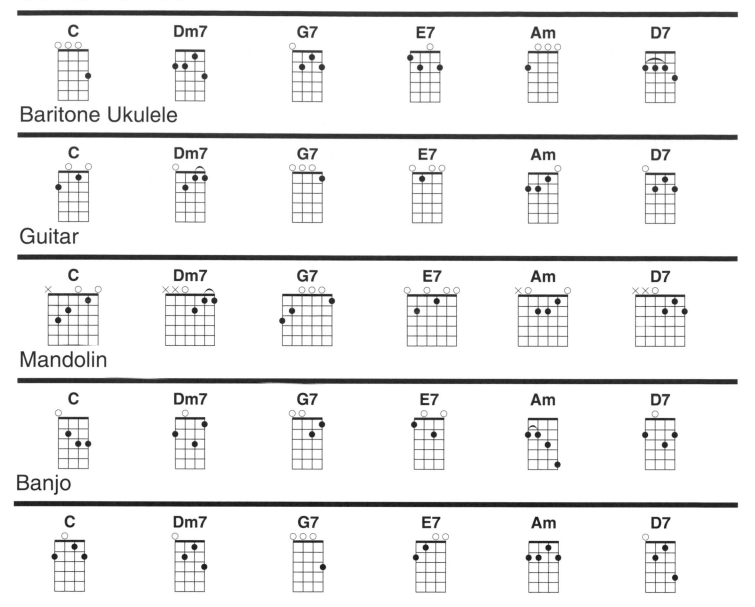

Rumbly in My Tumbly*

from THE MANY ADVENTURES OF WINNIE THE POOH

Words and Music by Richard M. Sherman and Robert B. Sherman

Standard Ukulele

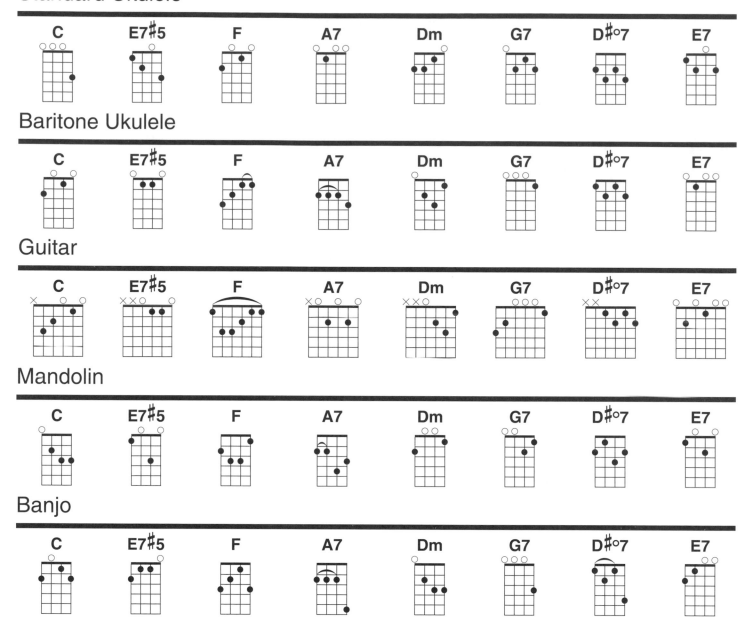

Baritone Ukulele

Guitar

Mandolin

Banjo

Some Day My Prince Will Come

from SNOW WHITE AND THE SEVEN DWARFS
Words by Larry Morey
Music by Frank Churchill

way   to   his   cas - tle   we'll   go _____   to   be

hap - py   for - ev - er,   I   know. _____

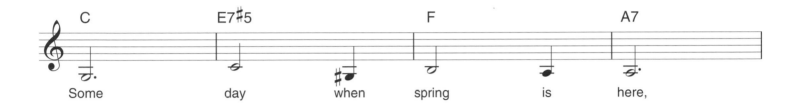

Some   day   when   spring   is   here,

we'll   find   our   love   a - new,   and   the

birds   will   sing   and   wed - ding   bells   will   ring   some

day   when   my   dreams   come   true. _____

Standard Ukulele

Baritone Ukulele

Guitar

Mandolin

Banjo

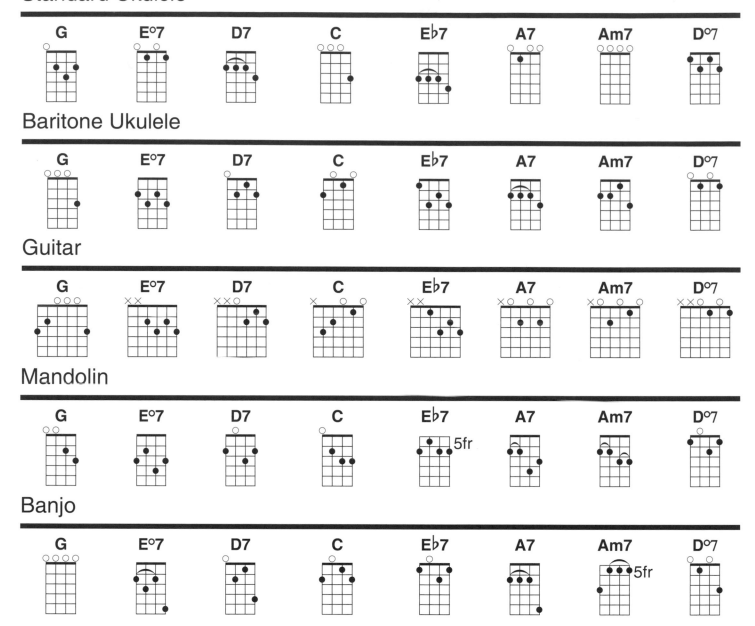

A Spoonful of Sugar

from MARY POPPINS

Words and Music by Richard M. Sherman and Robert B. Sherman

Verse

Moderately, in 2

1. In ev-'ry job that must be done there is an
   feath-er-ing his nest has ver-y
   bees that fetch the nec-tar from the

el-e-ment of fun. You find the fun and
lit-tle time to rest while gath-er-ing his
flow-ers to the comb nev-er tire of ev-er

snap, the job's a game. And ev'ry
bits of twine and twig. Though quite in -
buzz - ing to and fro be - cause they

task you un - der - take be - comes a piece of
tent in his pur - suit, he has a mer - ry tune to
take a lit - tle nip from ev - 'ry flow - er that they

cake, a lark! A spree! It's ver - y clear to
toot. He knows a song will move the job a -
sip, and hence, they find their task is not a

Chorus

see that
long, for } a spoon - ful of sug - ar helps the
grind, for

med - i - cine go down, the med - i - cine go down, ____

med - i - cine go down. Just a spoon - ful of sug - ar helps the

med - i - cine go down in a most de - light - ful

way. 2. A rob - in way. ____
    3. The hon - ey -

Standard Ukulele

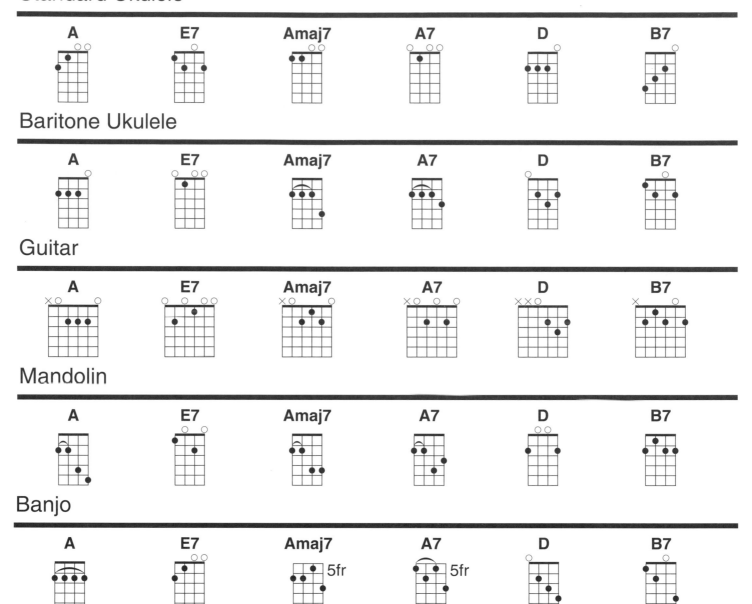

Baritone Ukulele

Guitar

Mandolin

Banjo

Supercalifragilisticexpialidocious

from MARY POPPINS
Words and Music by Richard M. Sherman and Robert B. Sherman

Chorus
Moderately fast, in 2

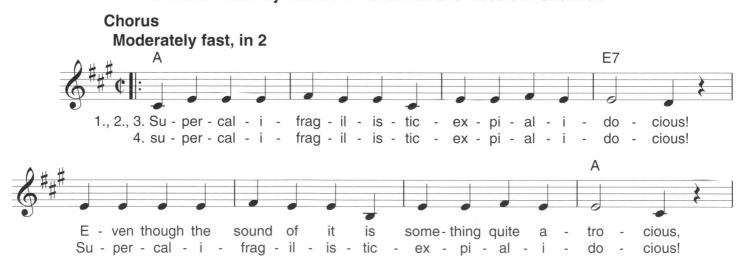

1., 2., 3. Su - per - cal - i - frag - il - is - tic - ex - pi - al - i - do - cious!
4. su - per - cal - i - frag - il - is - tic - ex - pi - al - i - do - cious!

E - ven though the sound of it is some - thing quite a - tro - cious,
Su - per - cal - i - frag - il - is - tic - ex - pi - al - i - do - cious!

Standard Ukulele

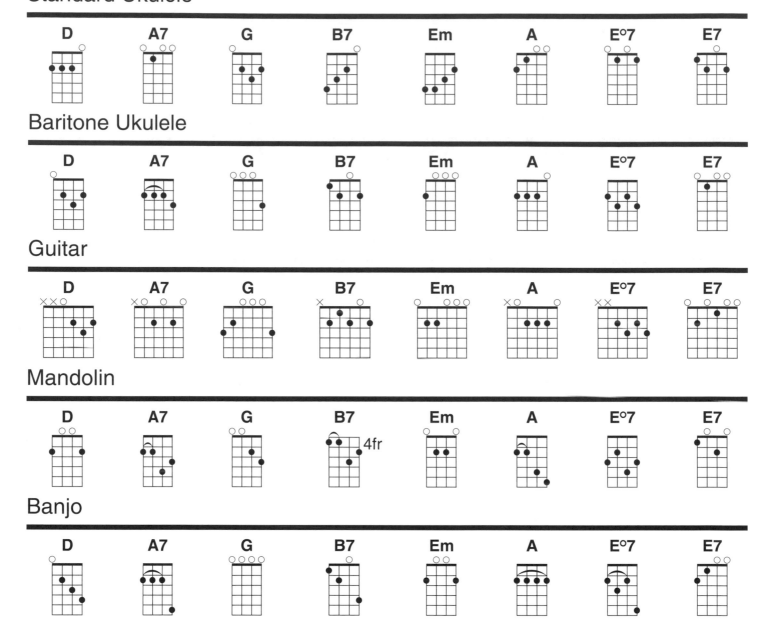

Baritone Ukulele

Guitar

Mandolin

Banjo

That's What Makes the World Go 'Round
from THE SWORD IN THE STONE
Words and Music by Richard M. Sherman and Robert B. Sherman

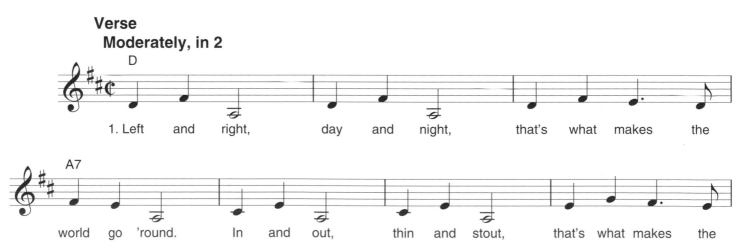

Verse
Moderately, in 2

D

1. Left and right, day and night, that's what makes the

A7

world go 'round. In and out, thin and stout, that's what makes the

Standard Ukulele

Baritone Ukulele

Guitar

Mandolin

Banjo

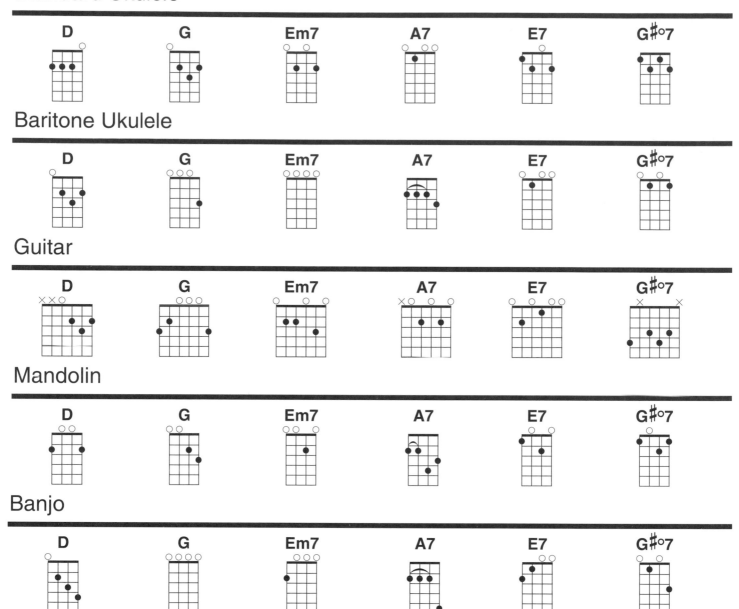

The Unbirthday Song

from ALICE IN WONDERLAND
Music by Mack David and Al Hoffman
Words by Jerry Livingston

Intro
Moderately fast, in 2

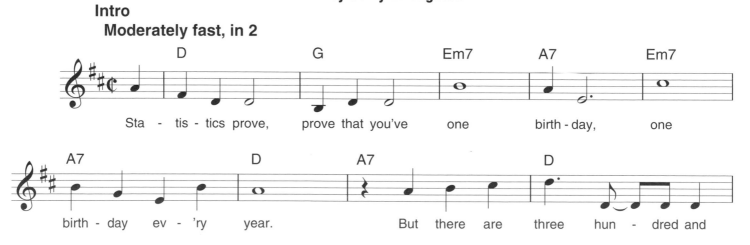

Sta - tis - tics prove, prove that you've one birth - day, one

birth - day ev - 'ry year. But there are three hun - dred and

six - ty - four   un -   birth - days;   that   is   why   we're

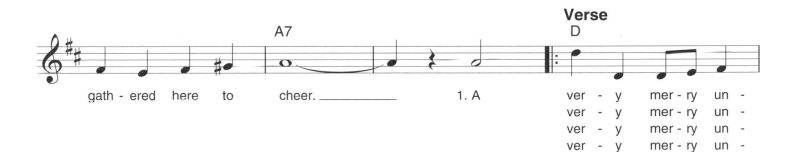

gath - ered   here   to   cheer. _____   1. A   ver - y   mer - ry   un -
                                                      ver - y   mer - ry   un -
                                                      ver - y   mer - ry   un -
                                                      ver - y   mer - ry   un -

Verse

birth - day   to   you,   to   you.   A   ver - y   mer - ry   un -
birth - day   to   us,   to   us.   A   ver - y   mer - ry   un -
birth - day   to   me.   (To   who?)   A   ver - y   mer - ry   un -
birth - day   to   all,   to   all.   A   ver - y   mer - ry   un -

birth - day   to   you,   to   you.   It's   great   to   drink   to
birth - day   to   us,   to   us.   If   there   are   no   ob -
birth - day   to   me.   (To   you?)   Let's   all   con - grat -   u -
birth - day   to   all,   to   all.   Let's   have   a   cel -   e -

some - one   and   I   guess   that   you   will   do.   A   ver - y   mer - ry   un -
jec - tions,   let   it   be   u -   nan - i -   mous. A   ver - y   mer - ry   un -
late   me   with   a   pres -   ent,   I   a -   gree. A   ver - y   mer - ry   un -
bra - tion,   hire   a   band   and   rent   a   hall. A   ver - y   mer - ry   un -

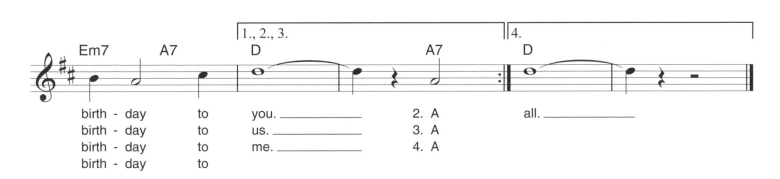

birth - day   to   you. _____   2. A   all. _____
birth - day   to   us. _____   3. A
birth - day   to   me. _____   4. A
birth - day   to

Standard Ukulele

Baritone Ukulele

Guitar

Mandolin

Banjo

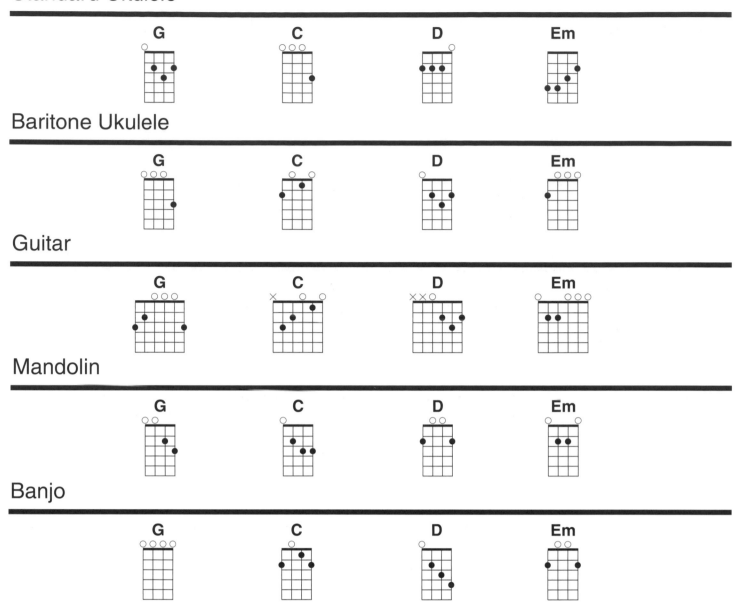

We Know the Way

from MOANA
Music by Opetaia Foa'i
Lyrics by Opetaia Foa'i and Lin-Manuel Miranda

Verse
Moderately

1. Ta - tou ta - ga - ta fo - lau   va - la - 'a - ui - na
2. We read the wind and the sky   when the sun is high.

e le a - tu - a. O le sa - mi te - le _____ e o mai
We sail the length of the seas ____ on the o - cean breeze.

la a-va-'e le lu-'i-tau e le-lei. _____ Ta-pe-na-pe-na._
At night we name ev-'ry star. _____ We know who we are, _

Chorus

_____ we know who we are, who we are. A-ue! A-ue!
we know who we are, who we are. A-way, a-way,

Nu-ku i mu-a. Te ma-nu-le-le e ta-
we set a course to find a brand new is-land ev-'ry-

ta-ki iei. A-ue! A-ue! Te fen-ua te mal-i-e.
where we roam. A-way, a-way, we keep our is-land in our mind,

1. Na-e ko ha-ki-li-a ka-i-ga e.
and when it's time to find home, **2.** we know the way. _____

Chorus

_____ We are ex-plor-ers read-ing ev-'ry sign. We tell the sto-ries of our
(A-way, a-way.)

eld-ers in a nev-er-end-ing chain. _____ Te fen-ua te mal-i-e.
(A-ue! A-ue!)

Na-e ko ha-ki-li-a. We know the way! _____

87

Standard Ukulele

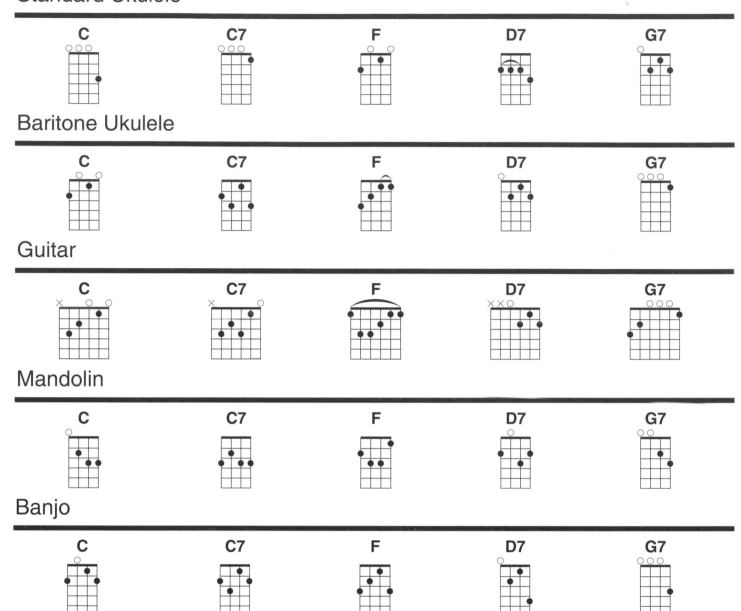

Baritone Ukulele

Guitar

Mandolin

Banjo

Westward Ho, the Wagons!

from WESTWARD HO, THE WAGONS!
Words by Tom Blackburn
Music by George Bruns

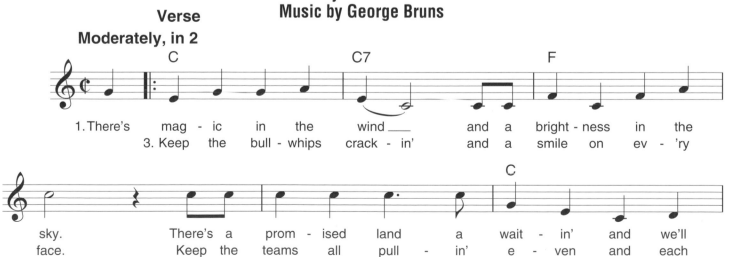

1. There's mag - ic in the wind ___ and a bright - ness in the
3. Keep the bull - whips crack - in' and a smile on ev - 'ry

sky. There's a prom - ised land a wait - in' and we'll
face. Keep the teams all pull - in' e - ven and each

Standard Ukulele

Baritone Ukulele

Guitar

Mandolin

Banjo

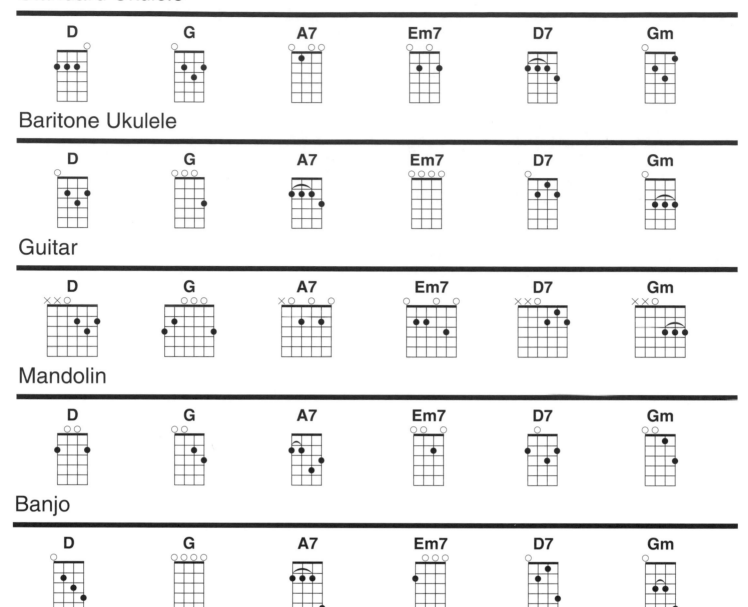

A Whale of a Tale

from 20,000 LEAGUES UNDER THE SEA

Words and Music by Norman Gimbel and Al Hoffman

𝄋 **Chorus**

Moderately, in 2

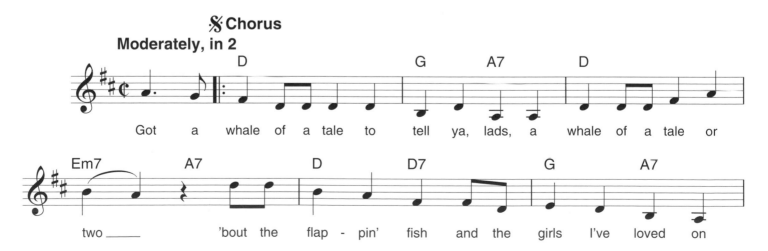

Got a whale of a tale to tell ya, lads, a whale of a tale or

two ___ 'bout the flap-pin' fish and the girls I've loved on

Standard Ukulele

Baritone Ukulele

Guitar

Mandolin

Banjo

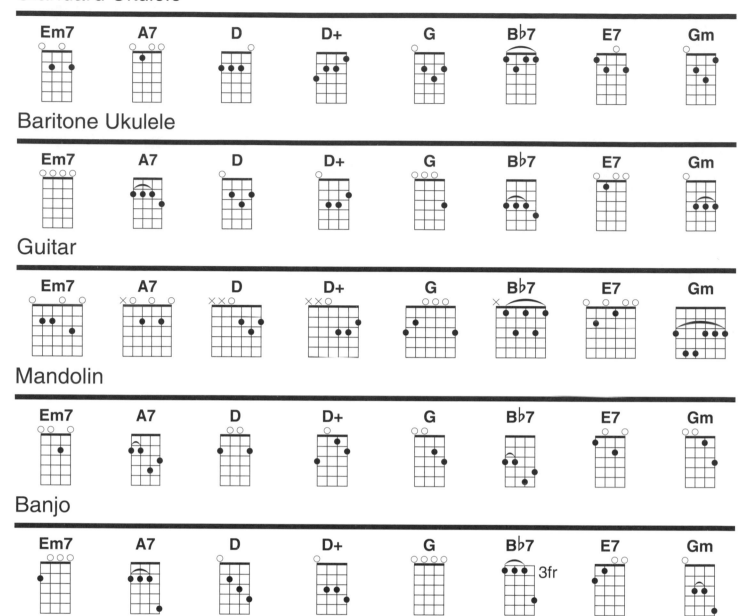

When I See an Elephant Fly

from DUMBO
Words by Ned Washington
Music by Oliver Wallace

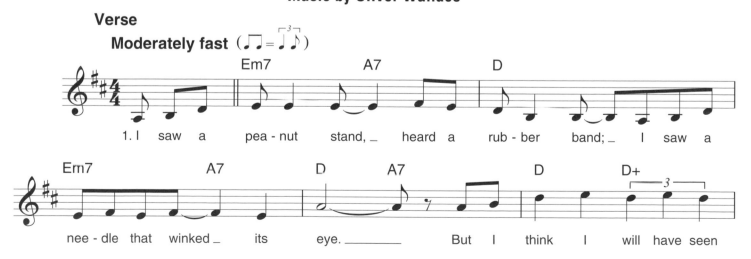

ev - 'ry - thing __ when I see an el - e - phant fly. 2. I saw a

Verse

front porch swing, __ heard a dia - mond ring; __ I saw a pol - ka dot rail - road

tie. _____ But I think I will have seen ev - 'ry - thing __ when

Bridge

I see an el - e - phant fly. I saw a clothes __ horse

rar' up and buck; __ they tell me that a man made a veg - 'ta - ble truck. __

I did - n't see __ that, I on - ly heard, __ but just to be so - cia - ble I'll

Verse

take their word, __ 3. I heard a fire - side chat, __ saw a base - ball bat, __ and I just

laughed till I thought __ I'd die. _____ But I think I will have seen

ev - 'ry - thing __ when I see an el - e - phant fly.

Standard Ukulele

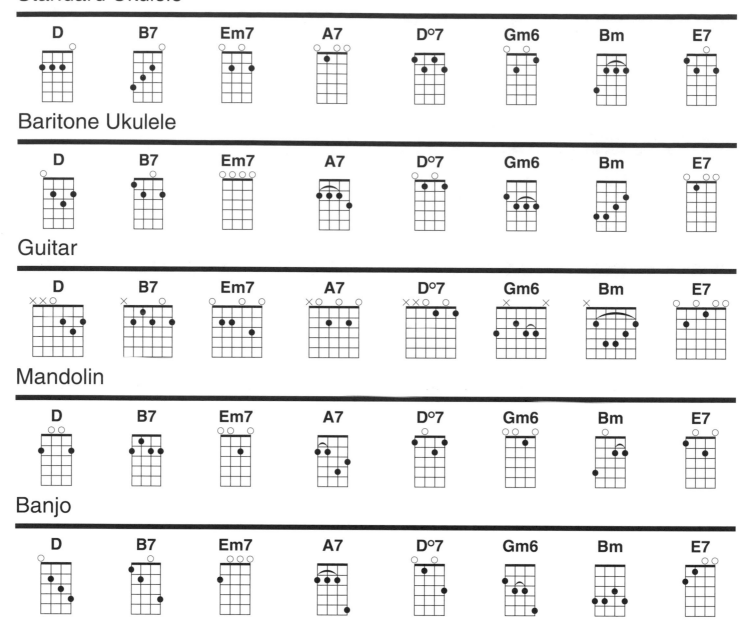

Baritone Ukulele

Guitar

Mandolin

Banjo

When You Wish Upon a Star

from PINOCCHIO
featured in THE WONDERFUL WORLD OF DISNEY
Words by Ned Washington
Music by Leigh Harline

Verse
Moderately

1. When you wish up - on a star, makes no dif - f'rence

who you are. An - y - thing your heart de - sires will

Standard Ukulele

Baritone Ukulele

Guitar

Mandolin

Banjo

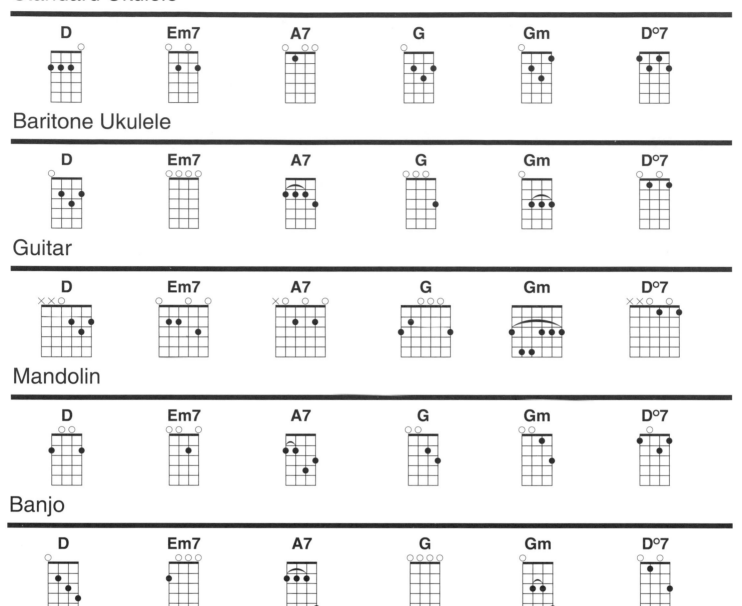

Whistle While You Work

from SNOW WHITE AND THE SEVEN DWARFS
Words by Larry Morey
Music by Frank Churchill

Verse
Moderately, in 2

1. Just whis - tle while you work. *Whistle:* _____

_____ And cheer - ful - ly to - geth - er we can

Standard Ukulele

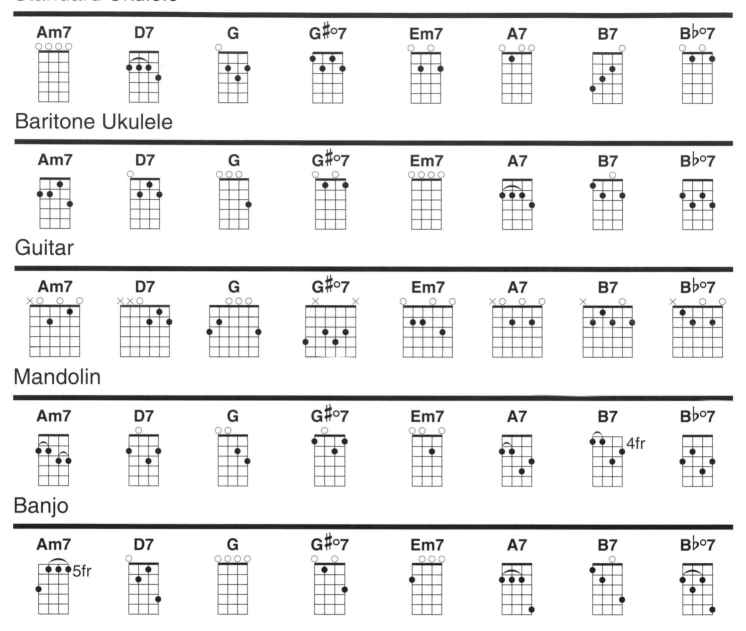

Baritone Ukulele

Guitar

Mandolin

Banjo

Winnie the Pooh*

from THE MANY ADVENTURES OF WINNIE THE POOH

Words and Music by Richard M. Sherman and Robert B. Sherman

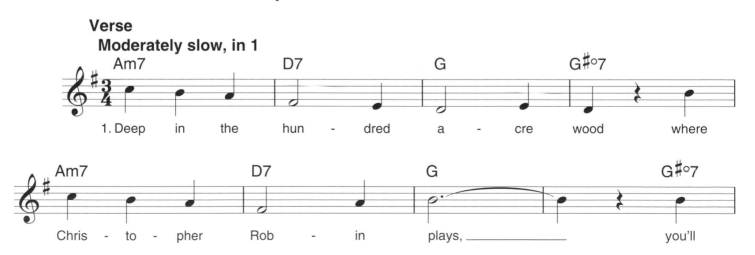

Verse
Moderately slow, in 1

1. Deep in the hun - dred a - cre wood where

Chris - to - pher Rob - in plays, _____ you'll

find the en - chant - ed neigh - bor - hood of

Chris - to - pher's child - hood days. _____ 2. A

Verse
Moderately
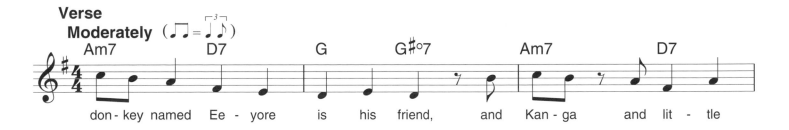
don - key named Ee - yore is his friend, and Kan - ga and lit - tle

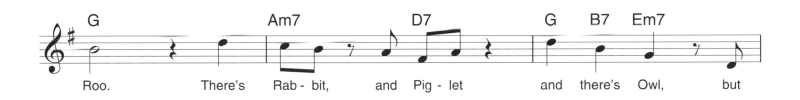
Roo. There's Rab - bit, and Pig - let and there's Owl, but

Chorus

most of all Win - nie the Pooh! Win - nie the Pooh, Win - nie the Pooh,

tub - by lit - tle cub - by all stuffed with fluff. He's Win - nie the Pooh,

Win - nie the Pooh, wil - ly, nil - ly, sil - ly ole bear.

Standard Ukulele

Baritone Ukulele

Guitar

Mandolin

Banjo

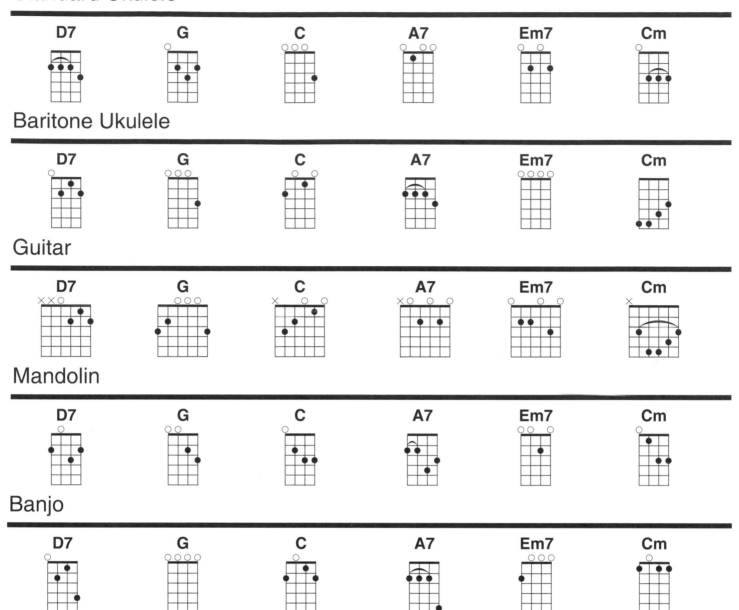

The Wonderful Thing About Tiggers*

from THE MANY ADVENTURES OF WINNIE THE POOH
Words and Music by Richard M. Sherman and Robert B. Sherman

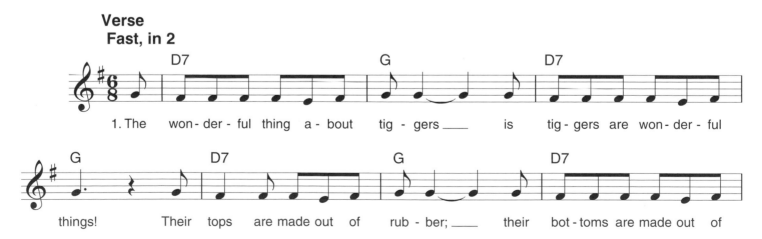

Verse
Fast, in 2

1. The won-der-ful thing a-bout tig-gers ___ is tig-gers are won-der-ful

things! Their tops are made out of rub-ber; ___ their bot-toms are made out of

Standard Ukulele

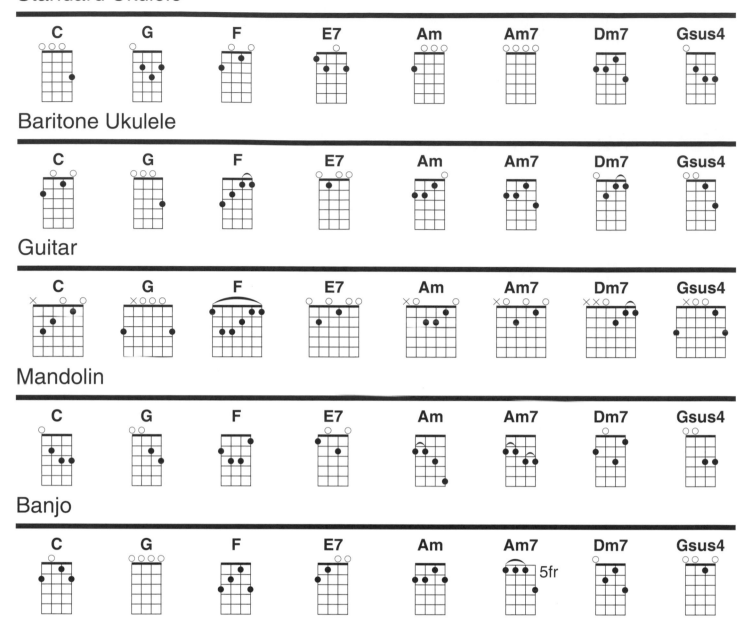

Baritone Ukulele

Guitar

Mandolin

Banjo

Written in the Stars

from AIDA

Music by Elton John
Lyrics by Tim Rice

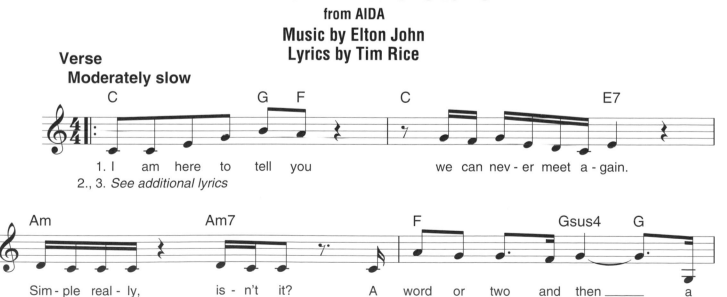

Verse
Moderately slow

1. I am here to tell you   we can nev-er meet a-gain.
2., 3. *See additional lyrics*

Sim-ple real-ly,   is-n't it?   A word or two and then _____ a

Additional Lyrics

2. Never wonder what I feel as living shuffles by.
You don't have to ask me and I need not reply.
Every moment of my life from now until I die,
I will think or dream of you and fail to understand
How a perfect love can be confounded out of hand.

3. Nothing can be altered; there is nothing to decide.
No escape, no change of heart nor any place to hide.
Oh, you are all I ever want, but this I am denied.
Sometimes in my darkest thoughts I wish I never learned
What it is to be in love and have that love returned.

Standard Ukulele

Baritone Ukulele

Guitar

Mandolin

Banjo

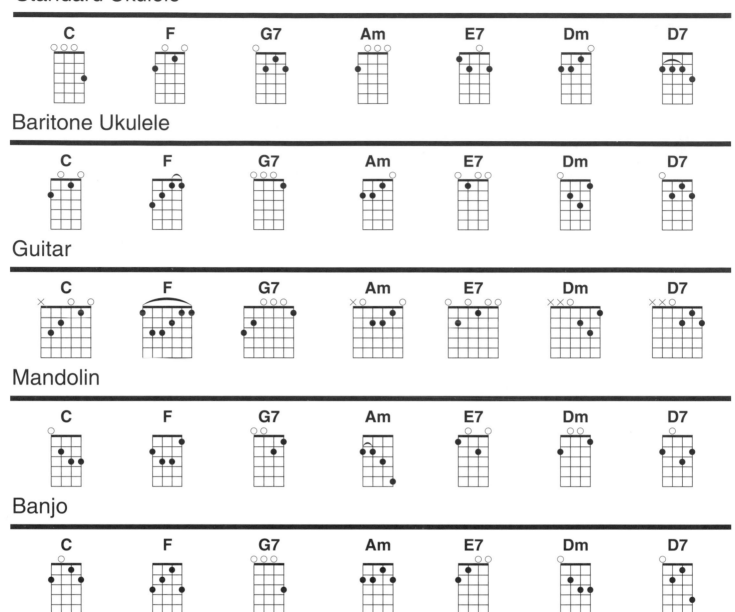

Yo Ho
(A Pirate's Life for Me)
from Disney Parks' Pirates of the Caribbean attraction
Words by Xavier Atencio
Music by George Bruns

up, me 'eart - ies, yo ho. We kid - nap and rav - age and

don't give a hoot. Drink up, me 'eart - ies, yo ho. ho. 4. We're

Verse

ras - cals, scoun - drels, vil - lains and knaves. Drink up, me 'eart - ies, yo

5. *See additional lyrics*

ho. We're dev - ils and black sheep, real - ly bad eggs. Drink

Chorus

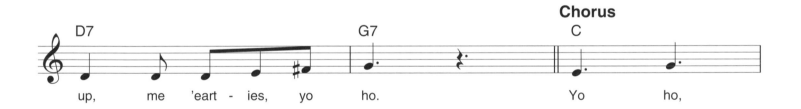

up, me 'eart - ies, yo ho. Yo ho,

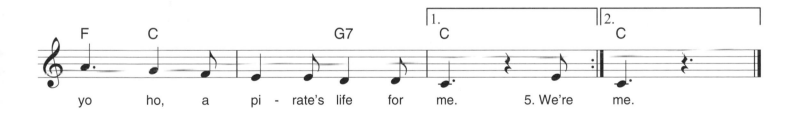

yo ho, a pi - rate's life for me. 5. We're me.

Additional Lyrics

2. We extort, we pilfer, we filch and sack.
   Drink up, me 'earties, yo ho.
   Maraud and embezzle and even highjack.
   Drink up, me 'earties, yo ho.

3. We kindle and char, inflame and ignite.
   Drink up, me 'earties, yo ho.
   We burn up the city; we're really a fright.
   Drink up, me 'earties, yo ho.

5. We're beggars and blighters and ne'er-do-well cads.
   Drink up, me 'earties, yo ho.
   Aye, but we're loved by our mommies 'n' dads.
   Drink up, me 'earties, yo ho.

Standard Ukulele

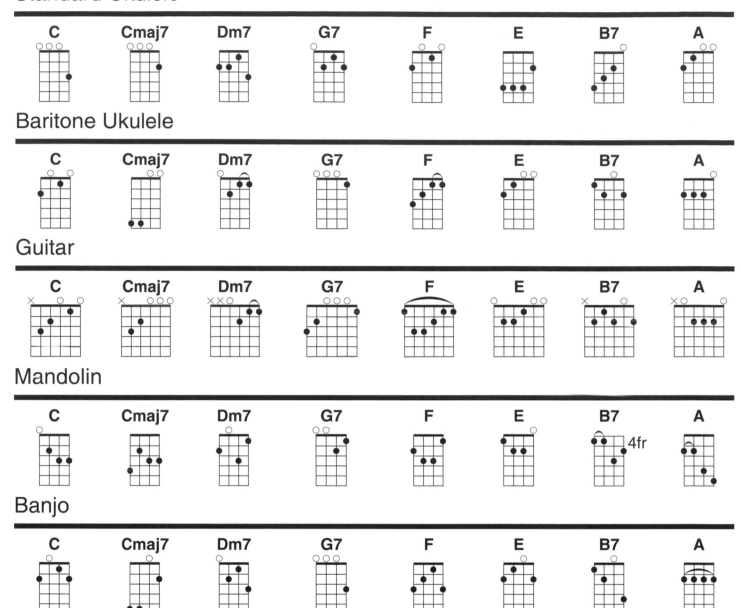

Baritone Ukulele

Guitar

Mandolin

Banjo

You Can Fly! You Can Fly! You Can Fly!

from PETER PAN

Words by Sammy Cahn

Music by Sammy Fain

Verse

Moderately, in 2

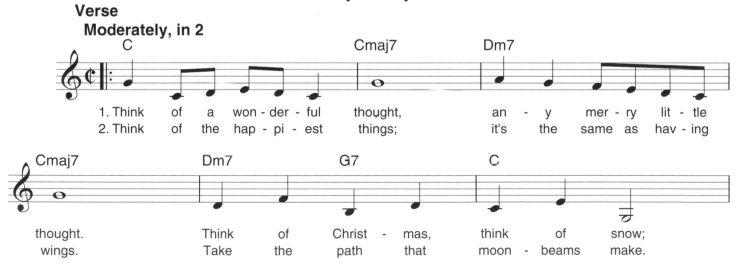

1. Think of a won-der-ful thought, an-y mer-ry lit-tle thought.
2. Think of the hap-pi-est things; it's the same as hav-ing wings.

thought. Think of Christ-mas, think of snow;
wings. Take the path that moon-beams make.

Standard Ukulele

Baritone Ukulele

Guitar

Mandolin

Banjo

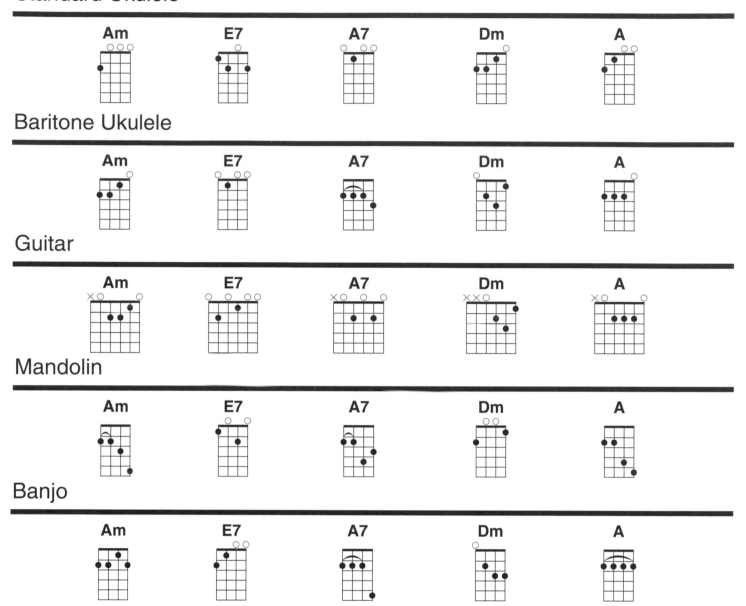

Theme from Zorro
from ZORRO
Words by Norman Foster
Music by George Bruns

Verse
Moderately, in 2

1. Out of the night, when the full moon is bright, comes the horse - man known as Zor - ro.

This bold ___ ren - e - gade carves a Z ___ with his blade, ___ a Z that stands for Zor - ro. ___

𝄋 Chorus

Zor - ro ___ the fox so cun - ning and free. ___

Zor - ro, ___ who makes the sign of the

Fine **Verse**

Z. ___ 2. He is po - lite, but the wick - ed take

flight ___ when they catch the sight of Zor - ro. ___

He's friend ___ of the weak and the poor ___ and the

D.S. al Fine

meek, this ver - y u - nique se - ñor Zor - ro. ___

Tuning

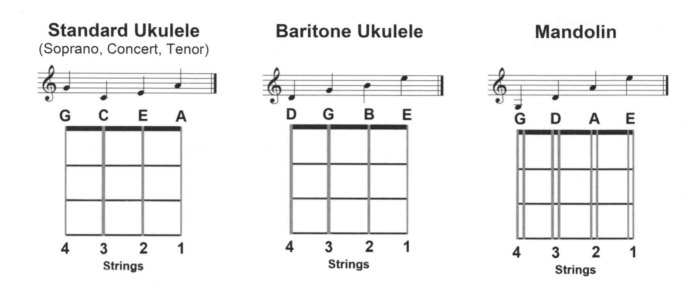

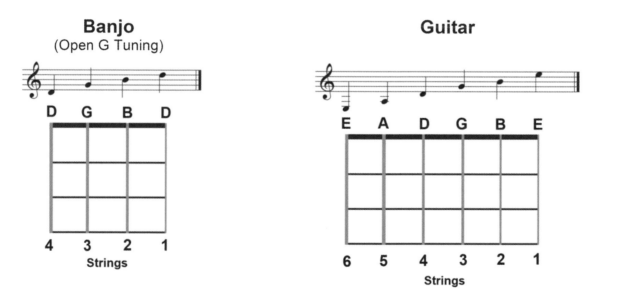

All banjo chord formations illustrated in this book are based on "Open G" tuning. If an alternate tuning is used the banjo player can read the chord letters for the songs and disregard the diagrams.

STRUM & SING

The Strum & Sing series for guitar and ukulele provides an unplugged and pared-down approach to your favorite songs – just the chords and the lyrics, with nothing fancy. These easy-to-play arrangements are designed for both aspiring and professional musicians.

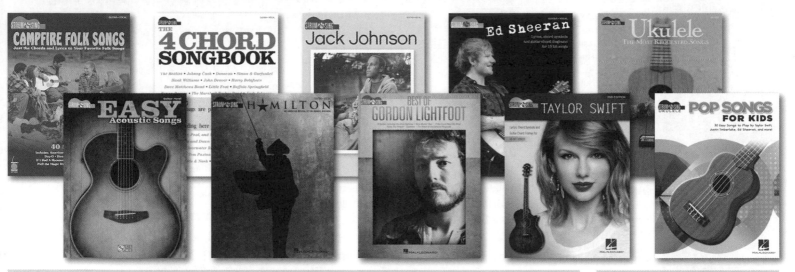

GUITAR

Acoustic Classics
00191891 ....$16.99

Adele
00159855 ....$12.99

Sara Bareilles
00102354 ....$12.99

The Beatles
00172234 ....$17.99

Blues
00159335 ....$12.99

Zac Brown Band
02501620 ....$19.99

Colbie Caillat
02501725 ....$14.99

Campfire Folk Songs
02500686 ....$15.99

Chart Hits of 2014-2015
00142554 ....$12.99

Chart Hits of 2015-2016
00156248 ....$12.99

Best of Kenny Chesney
00142457 ....$14.99

Christmas Carols
00348351 ....$14.99

Christmas Songs
00171332 ....$14.99

Kelly Clarkson
00146384 ....$14.99

Leonard Cohen
00265489 ....$16.99

Dear Evan Hansen
00295108 ....$16.99

John Denver Collection
02500632 ....$17.99

Disney
00233900 ....$17.99

Eagles
00157994 ....$14.99

Easy Acoustic Songs
00125478 ....$19.99

Billie Eilish
00363094 ....$14.99

The Five-Chord Songbook
02501718 ....$14.99

Folk Rock Favorites
02501669 ....$16.99

Folk Songs
02501482 ....$15.99

The Four-Chord Country Songbook
00114936 ....$16.99

The Four Chord Songbook
02501533 ....$14.99

Four Chord Songs
00249581 ....$16.99

The Greatest Showman
00278383 ....$14.99

Hamilton
00217116 ....$15.99

Jack Johnson
02500858 ....$19.99

Robert Johnson
00191890 ....$12.99

Carole King
00115243 ....$10.99

Best of Gordon Lightfoot
00139393 ....$15.99

John Mayer
02501636 ....$19.99

The Most Requested Songs
02501748 ....$19.99

Jason Mraz
02501452 ....$14.99

Tom Petty – Wildflowers & All the Rest
00362682 ....$14.99

Elvis Presley
00198890 ....$12.99

Queen
00218578 ....$12.99

Rock Around the Clock
00103625 ....$12.99

Rock Ballads
02500872 ....$12.99

Rocketman
00300469 ....$17.99

Ed Sheeran
00152016 ....$14.99

The Six-Chord Songbook
02502277 ....$17.99

Chris Stapleton
00362625 ....$19.99

Cat Stevens
00116827 ....$17.99

Taylor Swift
01191699 ....$19.99

The Three-Chord Songbook
00211634 ....$14.99

Top Christian Hits
00156331 ....$12.99

Top Hits of 2016
00194288 ....$12.99

The Who
00103667 ....$12.99

Yesterday
00301629 ....$14.99

Neil Young – Greatest Hits
00138270 ....$16.99

UKULELE

The Beatles
00233899 ....$16.99

Colbie Caillat
02501731 ....$10.99

Coffeehouse Songs
00138238 ....$14.99

John Denver
02501694 ....$17.99

The 4-Chord Ukulele Songbook
00114331 ....$16.99

Jack Johnson
02501702 ....$19.99

John Mayer
02501706 ....$10.99

The Most Requested Songs
02501453 ....$15.99

Pop Songs for Kids
00284415 ....$17.99

Sing-Along Songs
02501710 ....$17.99

HAL•LEONARD®

halleonard.com
Visit our website to see full song lists
or order from your favorite retailer.

*Prices, contents and availability
subject to change without notice.*

The Best Collections for Ukulele

The Best Songs Ever

70 songs have now been arranged for ukulele. Includes: Always • Bohemian Rhapsody • Memory • My Favorite Things • Over the Rainbow • Piano Man • What a Wonderful World • Yesterday • You Raise Me Up • and more.

00282413 . . . . $17.99

Campfire Songs for Ukulele

30 favorites to sing as you roast marshmallows and strum your uke around the campfire. Includes: God Bless the U.S.A. • Hallelujah • The House of the Rising Sun • I Walk the Line • Puff the Magic Dragon • Wagon Wheel • You Are My Sunshine • and more.

00129170 . . . . $15.99

The Daily Ukulele

arr. Liz and Jim Beloff
Strum a different song everyday with easy arrangements of 365 of your favorite songs in one big songbook! Includes favorites by the Beatles, Beach Boys, and Bob Dylan, folk songs, pop songs, kids' songs, Christmas carols, and Broadway and Hollywood tunes, all with a spiral binding for ease of use.

00240356 Original Edition $44.99
00240681 Leap Year Edition $44.99
00119270 Portable Edition $39.99

Disney Hits for Ukulele

Play 23 of your favorite Disney songs on your ukulele. Includes: The Bare Necessities • Cruella De Vil • Do You Want to Build a Snowman? • Kiss the Girl • Lava • Let It Go • Once upon a Dream • A Whole New World • and more.

00151250 . . . . $16.99

Also available:

00291547 Disney Fun Songs for Ukulele $17.99
00701708 Disney Songs for Ukulele $15.99
00334696 First 50 Disney Songs on Ukulele $22.99

First 50 Songs You Should Play on Ukulele

An amazing collec-tion of 50 accessible, must-know favorites: Edelweiss • Hey, Soul Sister • I Walk the Line • I'm Yours • Imagine • Over the Rainbow • Peaceful Easy Feeling • The Rainbow Connection • Riptide • more.

00149250 . . . . $19.99

Also available:

00292982 First 50 Melodies on Ukulele $16.99
00289029 First 50 Songs on Solo Ukulele $16.99
00347437 First 50 Songs to Strum on Uke $19.99

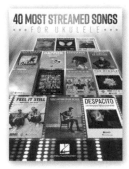

40 Most Streamed Songs for Ukulele

40 top hits that sound great on uke! Includes: Despacito • Feel It Still • Girls like You • Happier • Havana • High Hopes • The Middle • Perfect • 7 Rings • Shallow • Shape of You • Something Just like This • Stay • Sucker • Sunflower • Sweet but Psycho • Thank U, Next • There's Nothing Holdin' Me Back • Without Me • and more!

00298113 . . . . $17.99

The 4 Chord Songbook

With just 4 chords, you can play 50 hot songs on your ukulele! Songs include: Brown Eyed Girl • Do Wah Diddy Diddy • Hey Ya! • Ho Hey • Jessie's Girl • Let It Be • One Love • Stand by Me • Toes • With or Without You • and many more.

00142050 . . . . $17.99

Also available:

00141143 The 3-Chord Songbook $17.99

Pop Songs for Kids

30 easy pop favorites for kids to play on uke, including: Brave • Can't Stop the Feeling! • Feel It Still • Fight Song • Happy • Havana • House of Gold • How Far I'll Go • Let It Go • Remember Me (Ernesto de la Cruz) • Rewrite the Stars • Roar • Shake It Off • Story of My Life • What Makes You Beautiful • and more.

00284415 . . . . $17.99

Simple Songs for Ukulele

50 favorites for standard G-C-E-A ukulele tuning, including: All Along the Watchtower • Can't Help Falling in Love • Don't Worry, Be Happy • Ho Hey • I'm Yours • King of the Road • Sweet Home Alabama • You Are My Sunshine • and more.

00156815 . . . . $15.99

Also available:

00276644 More Simple Songs for Ukulele $14.99

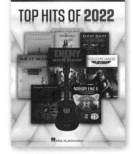

Top Hits of 2022

This collection features 16 of today's top hits arranged with vocal melody, lyrics, and chord diagrams for standard G-C-E-A tuning for ukulele. Songs include: As It Was • Bam Bam • Carolina • Enemy • Freedom • Glimpse of Us • Hold My Hand • Light Switch • Love Me More • Nobody like U • Numb Little Bug • On My Way • Running up That Hill • and more.

01100312 . . . . $14.99

Also available:

00355553 Top Hits of 2020 . . . . $14.99
00302274 Top Hits of 2019 . . . . $14.99

Ukulele: The Most Requested Songs

Strum & Sing Series
Cherry Lane Music
Nearly 50 favorites all expertly arranged for ukulele! Includes: Bubbly • Build Me Up Buttercup • Cecilia • Georgia on My Mind • Kokomo • L-O-V-E • Your Body Is a Wonderland • and more.

02501453 . . . . $15.99

The Ultimate Ukulele Fake Book

Uke enthusiasts will love this giant, spiral-bound collection of over 400 songs for uke! Includes: Crazy • Dancing Queen • Downtown • Fields of Gold • Happy • Hey Jude • 7 Years • Summertime • Thinking Out Loud • Thriller • Wagon Wheel • and more.

00175500 9" x 12" Edition $45.00
00319997 5.5" x 8.5" Edition $39.99